GET USED TO

DIF
FER
ENT

STUDENT GUIDE

GET USED TO DIFFERENT
Published by David C Cook
4050 Lee Vance Drive
Colorado Springs, CO 80918 U.S.A.

Integrity Music Limited, a Division of David C Cook
Brighton, East Sussex BN1 2RE, England

The graphic circle C logo is a registered trademark of David C Cook.

ISBN 978-0-8307-8475-2
eISBN 978-0-8307-8476-9

The Team: Michael Covington, Stephanie Bennett, James Hershberger,
Justin Claypool, Brian Mellema, Jack Campbell, Susan Murdock

Printed in the United States of America
First Edition 2024

1 2 3 4 5 6 7 8 9 10

101623

Contents

Part 3: Bringing Your Burdens to Jesus

Week 7

Week 8

Week 9

Introduction

I was fifteen when I found out my sister was actually my mom.

Yeah, you read that right.

I remember precisely where I was when I heard the news—in the passenger seat of a car heading north on Alpine Road. I don't remember much after that … other than going straight to the closet in my room, closing the door behind me, and crying for hours.

My brothers were now, biologically, my uncles. My other sisters were really my aunts. My parents were actually … my grandparents? Turns out, they had decided to take care of me as an infant, hoping my teenage mother struggling with addiction would someday be able to raise me. When it became clear she wasn't going to, they adopted me as their son.

In one split second in that car on Alpine Road, my entire identity crumbled. A teen who felt accepted or even "normal"? I wish. An ambitious student chasing good grades? Not anymore. The big, tough captain of the football team? Hardly.

I'd love to tell you my faith was a magic wand that made all the pain go away—that it somehow solved my problems. But, as you know, that's not how life really works.

This book is about what **does** work: finding your identity in Jesus and following Him, even when your world falls apart. In the following pages, you'll find three sections that each correspond to a season of **The Chosen**. In part 1, we'll look at what identity means in today's complicated world. In part 2, we'll unpack Jesus's blueprint for everyday living. In part 3, we'll ask tough questions about pain and suffering.

While it wasn't a magic wand, following Jesus absolutely made the difference in my life because it made **me** different. Jesus restored my identity. He taught me how to live. He walked alongside me through the pain.

My hope is through Scripture, the show, and this book, you will learn what it means to

Get Used
to Different

— Jeremiah Smith

Part 1

Finding Your Identity in Jesus

1

Who You Are

Maybe you've gone to church your whole life. Maybe you've never been. Maybe you're reading this with a group of friends. Maybe you're reading it alone. Maybe you consider Jesus someone worth following. Maybe your Aunt Linda gave you this book and these are the only words you'll ever read from it.

Maybe you're happy. Maybe you had a hard time even getting out of bed this morning. Maybe you're confident. Maybe you just want to be noticed. Maybe you do well in school. Maybe school is the last place you want to be. Maybe you've got concrete goals and your future clearly laid out. Maybe you have no idea what you're going to do today, much less what you want to be when you grow up.

Maybe you're tall. Maybe you're short. Maybe you feel too fat. Maybe you feel too skinny. Maybe you're great at sports. Maybe you dread P.E. Maybe you're homeschooled and have no idea what P.E. even stands for. Maybe you've been bullied. Maybe you're the bully and don't realize it. Maybe you're in love. Maybe that person doesn't feel the same and your heart aches because of it.

Maybe you've got perfect skin. Maybe you're embarrassed by your clothes. Maybe you're popular. Maybe no one understands you. Maybe you're part of the cool crowd. Maybe you'd do anything for just one friend. Maybe you're loved dearly by your family. Maybe this isn't the first foster home you've been in. Maybe you've got what the school counselors call a "positive self-image." Maybe you have no idea what to think about yourself at all.

Scan to watch this clip!

Maybe, maybe, maybe, maybe, maybe …

The Chosen opened episode 1 with a little girl who had yet to experience her maybes. All she knew was the love of her father. It was clear she felt adored by him. Cherished. Treasured.

But then something happened. When we saw her again, we weren't even sure it was her. She was all grown up and going by a different name—Lilith—and her story wasn't easy to watch. How could a little girl, once so dearly loved by her father, end up on top of a cliff, ready to jump?

Maybe his illness left her alone as a child. Maybe she was abused as a result. Maybe she made mistakes because of all the hurt and the pain. Maybe she felt unlovable. Maybe she thought she was irredeemable. Maybe she grew so tired of struggling that she decided to give up.

Maybe, maybe, maybe.

When Jesus showed up at the end of the episode, He did something completely unexpected. Something no one had done in years: He called her by her real name.

"Mary," He said. **"Mary of Magdala."**

It was so specific. How would He—no, how **could** He—know her name?

"Thus says the Lord who created you, and He who formed you …"

It was the same verse her father used to read to her all those years ago. The same verse she had written down and kept so close.

"Fear not, for I have redeemed you."

With so many women in the Bible named Mary, this one was distinguished by her hometown of Magdala, which was a fishing village on the Sea of Galilee.

Up until that moment, she didn't know redemption was even possible.

"I have called you by name. You are Mine."

Turned out, she wasn't alone. Or forgotten. Rather, she was seen and known and pursued by the One who made her. And in that moment, Mary's maybes began to fade.

Truth is, we all spend a lot of time struggling with our identity, with who we really are. Unfortunately, trying to figure it out by ourselves often leads to one place: the edge of the cliff. But, like Mary's, that's not where our stories have to end because **Jesus is there too.** And when we turn around, we can see Him, ready to embrace us and remind us that, with Him, there are no more maybes.

Pray

God, thank You for not leaving me at the edge of the cliff. You created the entire universe, but You also created me. And You call me by name. ME. I don't exactly understand it yet, but thank You. Help me learn what it means to belong to You.

Reflect

1. How do you think Mary would list her maybes? What do you think others would say about her list?

2. What are **your** maybes?

3. What do you think it means that God calls you by name too?

2

Whose You Are

Here are a few more verses from Isaiah 43, the passage of Scripture Jesus quoted to Mary at the end of episode 1:

> Thus says the LORD,
> he who created you …
>   he who formed you …
> "Fear not, for I have redeemed you;
>   I have called you by name,
>   **you are mine.**
>
> When you pass through the waters, I will be with you;
>   and through the rivers, they shall not overwhelm
>   you;
> when you walk through fire you shall not be burned,
>   and the flame shall not consume you.
>
> For I am the LORD your God,
>   the Holy One of Israel, your Savior.
> I give Egypt as your ransom,
>   Cush and Seba in exchange for you."

Season 1,
Episode 1

That last part might sound a little weird, but it's extremely important—God was declaring that His people are highly valued. They are worth any price. He delivered the Israelites from their enemies (Egypt, Cush, and Seba) because even the wealth of nations can't compare to how much He values His people.

How much He values **you**.

But let's be honest. You don't always **feel** valued. It might be as simple as a joke made repeatedly at your expense or as complicated as a parent's disappointment. Sometimes those little aches and injuries add up. Sometimes the big hurts you face in life (and, yeah, there are a lot of them) make you feel like you're drowning, like you're passing through deep waters. Of course, our tendency is to focus on the water as it rises around us.

Hold on to that thought for a minute.

We've been told our entire lives that we need to find our own self-worth—that we must look within ourselves to find value. After all, no one knows us better than we know ourselves. It's up to us as individuals to find inner peace and self-acceptance.

So we're told, anyway.

When we can't quite find self-worth on our own, the culture offers a solution: self-help. Chances are you've been given plenty of advice about self-help, usually from well-intentioned people. Heck, a simple search turns up thousands of books, podcasts, and YouTube videos on the subject.

> Self-help:
> the use of one's own efforts and resources to achieve things without relying on others.

But no amount of self-help can restore self-worth.

Don't worry, though. The culture offers even more ways to regain your sense of control and help you feel better: eat more, work out more, play video games more, study more, use drugs more, daydream more, watch TikTok more, smoke more, plan more, travel more, hang

out with friends more, stream TV more, set goals more, sleep more, party more, post more, drink more, swipe more, go out more.

But while these activities might help you feel better for a moment, like most medicines, the effects always wear off. There's a word for that too: self-medication.

Self-worth > self-help > self-medication. It's an endless cycle—like a tiny little hamster stuck on a very large wheel. And running on a wheel is exhausting and stupid because it doesn't get you where you want to go.

So, how can you break the self-cycle?

"Fear not," Jesus told Mary. "For I have redeemed you. I have called you by name …" Then He said three words that—if you embrace them—will change the way you feel about yourself and everyone and everything around you: **"You are Mine."**

You belong to God even though every single day you're told the opposite because you live in a world that preaches you belong to yourself.

But here's the beautiful truth: Your value doesn't lie in who you are. **Your value lies in whose you are.** God created and formed you. He will show you your value. He will declare your worth. He will save you when the waters rise. He will hold back the flames so you're not burned.

Because you belong **not to yourself** but to God.

Pray

Father, help me find my worth in You, not in myself. You created me. You formed me. You have called me by name and You redeem me. Help me break this cycle and get off the hamster wheel.

Reflect

1. Describe how trying to find self-worth is an endless cycle.

2. How do you self-medicate? (Remember, not all of these activities are bad, but it's easy to use them to cover up negative feelings.)

3. What do you think it means to belong to God? How would your life be different if you got your self-worth directly from Him?

God's Way vs. Your Way

For being such a simple fisherman, Simon was complicated. We actually know a lot about him—probably more than any other disciple. We know he was married and that Jesus healed his mother-in-law (Matthew 8:14–15). We know that in a huge demonstration of faith, he actually walked on water to Jesus (14:28–29). We also know that Jesus gave Simon a new name—Peter—because he would be the "rock" on which Christ's church would be built (16:18). And after Jesus's death and resurrection, we know Simon Peter traveled far and wide spreading the good news about how others could be saved too (check out the New Testament book of Acts!).

Peter means ROCK in the Greek language.

But when you met Simon in **The Chosen**, he didn't really seem like disciple material. Instead, he was street-fighting, gambling, and cheating. His personal life wasn't much better. There was tension at home and he was at risk of losing the fishing business he had built with his brother, Andrew. And all of that caused him to do a very Simon-like thing:

He took matters into his own hands.

Like Simon, we can be incredibly stubborn sometimes. **I'll do it my way**, we think. **I know what's best for me.** Regardless of how many times things don't go the way we plan, and no matter how lousy we feel afterward, we do it again and again. We're like Simon after a night of fishing—exhausted from all our effort, feeling the pain that comes with it, and left with nothing to show for it.

Because taking matters into your own hands usually leaves you empty-handed.

But then, Jesus shows up. And He teaches you how to do things His way.

For Simon, you know what came next: the net broke, everyone yelled in a mix of disbelief and excitement, and another boat had to help pull in the miraculous catch. Which meant, the empty-handed fisherman suddenly had his hands full with more fish than he could count.

Season 1, Episode 4

What matters are you taking into your own hands? You can probably think of a few, but chances are, there's even more than that. Because while we're pretty good at inviting Jesus into our proverbial house, we usually don't want Him to see **every** room. So, we hold on to things in our lives a little tighter. Sometimes it's a behavior, like a habit that's hard to break. Or maybe we don't actually want to break the habit because we like it, even though we know it's not good for us. Often, we try to take relationships into our own hands, whether it's the kids we hang out with or the ones we give our hearts to.

Proverbial: not literal; a reference to a familiar saying. In other words, we want Jesus to come into our lives, but we don't want to include Him in every aspect of our lives.

Bottom line: even after Jesus enters our lives, we still want to do things our way.

Simon was like that too. Following Jesus didn't automatically fix his recklessness. Yes, he walked on water, but he also started sinking when he took his eyes **off** Jesus. And despite the new name of Peter, he still did crazy things like cutting off a man's ear (Matthew 26:51) and denying Jesus three times (26:69–75).

Following Jesus isn't a magic wand that will make your problems instantly go away. But here's the difference between doing things your way and doing things His way:

Jesus won't leave you empty-handed.

Pray

Father, I want to believe that Your way is best, but that's hard to do sometimes. There are so many things I hold on to, so many things I want to control. I'm afraid to let go. Help me break my sinful habits. Lead me into healthy relationships, and give me the strength to follow You. Help me stop taking matters into my own hands. Help me trust You enough to do things Your way.

Reflect

1. In what way(s) do you relate to Simon?

2. Do you think Jesus's way is better than your own? It's OK to be honest. What are some things you're still unsure about?

3. What habits or relationships do you need to stop doing your way and, instead, entrust to Jesus?

Accepted Already

4

Your identity (who you are, who you want to be, who you could become) is under constant attack. You feel it, don't you? Those little self-doubts. That second (or twentieth) look in the mirror.

Sometimes it's a small, quiet voice that keeps nagging at the back of your mind. Other times it's a roaring lion, clawing its way through your thoughts and emotions with the message that you just don't measure up. You fear that if people knew you, the real you, they'd turn the other way. Or, even worse, they'd laugh at you. Maybe they already do.

You're not alone. When we met Matthew in **The Chosen**, it was pretty clear he wouldn't have been allowed to sit at the cool kids' table, despite the fact that he wore the nicest clothes, had the biggest house, and could afford to throw away his sandals when they got a little … messy.

Bottom line: Matthew didn't fit in.

He was probably the smartest guy in town too. Being a tax collector was all about crunching numbers and doing the math no one else could.

But he didn't fit in.

The Romans, who had conquered Israel and ruled over the Jews, found what Matthew did incredibly valuable—and he was exceptionally good at his job. They even assigned him a personal guard.

But he didn't fit in.

His own people, the Jews, despised him so much that they spit on him when he walked by. His mother loved him but didn't know what to say to him. And his father … well, his father wanted nothing to do with him.

But then Jesus showed up and said two little words that changed everything:

Follow Me.

Season 1, Episode 7

In the Bible, the real-life Matthew didn't tell us much about his personal reasons for choosing to follow Jesus: "As Jesus passed on from there, he saw a man called Matthew sitting at the tax booth, and he said to him, 'Follow me.' And he rose and followed him" (Matthew 9:9).

But, reading on, we see that Jesus hung out with other tax collectors too. In other words, not just one outcast but a whole slew of 'em. The next verse in the Bible says that many sinners came and reclined with Jesus and His disciples.

Tax collectors and sinners—which meant they were definitely **not** sitting at the cool kids' table. In fact, Jesus's behavior was so scandalous, the religious leaders threw a fit. One of many to follow.

Soak that in for a minute. Here was the promised Messiah the Jews had been waiting for, and who did He choose to hang out with?

Well, you.

He chooses to hang out with you.

He knows every self-doubt you have. He sees those extra looks in the mirror. He hears the little voices (and the loud ones too) telling you that you don't measure up, no matter where you sit in the lunchroom.

> Messiah:
> the promised deliverer
> of the Jewish nation;
> another word for "Savior."

He sees you in your makeshift tax collector booth—that fortress you've made for yourself where you hide. But Jesus doesn't just walk by. As He did with Matthew, He stops. He looks at you. And He says two words that change everything:

"Follow Me."

Pray

Father, I have a confession to make. Even as I pray this prayer, I don't feel like I measure up. It's so easy to look at everyone else and see how much better they are than me. Yet You see me, right here in my tax collector booth. Thank You for being the God of tax collectors and everyone else who doesn't fit in. Help me keep the whispers of self-doubt from turning into a roar. Help me follow You, and no one and nothing else.

Reflect

1. In **The Chosen**, Matthew's character is portrayed as being on the autism spectrum. Why is that significant? What does this tell you about Jesus?

2. In what ways do you feel like you don't measure up, like you don't quite fit in?

3. Jesus is asking you to follow Him. What's your personal tax collector booth? Why is it hard to leave behind?

GUIDED GROUP DISCUSSION

1. We spend a lot of time struggling with our identity—with how others perceive us as well as how we perceive ourselves. Often, we look to our activities or accomplishments to define us. "I'm an athlete." "I'm a dancer." "I'm a good student." "I have a lot of followers on social media." But according to Isaiah 43:1, "Fear not, for I have redeemed you; I have called you by name, you are mine," what simple truth does God want us to place our identity in?

2. Self-help is the use of our own efforts and resources to accomplish things (including feeling "good") without depending on others. Self-worth is our sense of value or self-esteem. Self-medication is the act of treating ourselves in our own wisdom and without the advice of others.

Self

SELF

SELF!

Why do you think self-focus has failed so miserably to make us feel truly safe, valued, and cared for? What does Isaiah 43:2 say about how God cares for His people in the midst of hard things? (Of course, most of us won't actually have to endure literal floods or raging fires. But there are plenty of other circumstances that make us feel overwhelmed and overpowered.)

"When you pass through the waters, I will be with you; and through
the rivers, they shall not overwhelm you; when you walk through fire
you shall not be burned, and the flame shall not consume you."
Isaiah 43:2

3. One of the reasons we hear so much about self-help is because
we prefer doing things our own way. But to follow Jesus, we have to
do things His way. That's the thing about following: we are no longer
leading.

Duh.

So, what would it look like to follow God and focus on Him instead of
yourself? How would it change the way you feel about the hard things
in your life? What would change—like, actually change—if you truly
grasped how much God loves you?

"For I am the LORD your God, the Holy One of Israel, your Savior. I
give Egypt as your ransom, Cush and Seba in exchange for you."
Isaiah 43:3

(Don't get sidetracked by the names. God was simply illustrating how
far He's willing to go to bring His people to Himself. That He pursues His
people at any cost and with unrelenting mercy and grace.)

5

Who You're Looking For

There's a lot to learn from Jesus's conversation with the woman at the well. Stop here and read the full story in John chapter 4. It's a little long (forty-five verses!), but it's full of great stuff.

In fact, if you were reading this story in the first century, at least three things would've immediately jumped off the page. First, people from Samaria were outcasts and the Jews looked down on them. Second, this woman was an outcast **even from the outcasts**. Third, it would've been scandalous for **any** man to be at a well talking to this woman, let alone a religious teacher.

But that's exactly where we find Jesus.

Season 1,
Episode 8

In **The Chosen**, we understand these details through Photina's eyes (that's the name of the woman at the well in the show). We're able to see her, not just as another Bible character we learn about in youth group, but as a real person. Someone who lived a life full of heartbreak and loss: five husbands, a ton of rejection, and when Jesus entered the scene, living with a new guy who wasn't her husband.

She was clearly looking for … **something**. But no matter how many places she searched, no matter how many husbands she took, she was left wanting more. Which was why Jesus said to her, "Everyone who drinks of this water will be thirsty again, but whoever drinks of the water that I will give him will never be thirsty again" (John 4:13–14).

Once she found Jesus, she was done looking. And here's the point:

God is who you're looking for, even when you're looking everywhere else.

So, where are you looking? It's not hard to figure it out—just check your internet search history. Of course, like Photina, we prefer to go incognito, pretending we're not really looking **there**. Sometimes we even cover our tracks to hide where we've been.

Incognito: hiding your true identity or actions.

Or take a moment to consider how you spend your time. Or what you spend time thinking about. Remember that little hamster on the wheel? Like him, we go round and round, eating/dieting, practicing/playing, resting/partying, friending/isolating—and whatever else we do to self-medicate. Of course, the things we fill our days with aren't always "bad" … unless they keep us from the One we should be looking for. Because no matter how much water you drink from any kind of well, you're gonna be thirsty again.

And again and again and again. And again.

Looking. Thirsting. Searching.

Jesus went to the well intentionally. He knew who He'd find there. He was, in fact, looking for her—the outcast of outcasts. And once she met Jesus, she was done looking in all the wrong places because she had found what her soul was searching for.

Like her, you can stop looking everywhere else.

Jesus is already there, looking for you.

Pray

God, You're looking for me. And I'm looking for You, but I'm not always looking in the right places. I've got some hurts and hang-ups. Instead of trying to find You, I fill the empty space inside me with so many other things besides You. But You're looking for me and I want to look for You today, right now, in the right places.

Reflect

1. Where is your "everywhere else"? In other words, where are the places you go instead of straight to Jesus?

2. Why do you think Jesus went looking for the woman from Samaria?

3. Why does it matter that Jesus is looking for you and not just waiting for you to find Him?

6

Before and After

Luke 8:1–3 tells us that "Mary, called Magdalene, from whom seven demons had gone out" was one of the women traveling with Jesus and the twelve disciples. Luke doesn't tell us how or why seven demons had taken up residency inside her—it was just a statement of fact.

Before she met Jesus, she was **one way**.

Season 1, Episode 2

The Chosen portrays what life might've been like for Mary. She had every reason to be a mess. And, honestly, she had every reason to stay that way. Not that she wanted to, but life hadn't been kind to her and she responded the only way she knew how. That is, until Jesus showed up and changed everything.

After Jesus, she was completely different.

What's your "I was one way" story? We all have one. Like Mary's, some are born of trauma. Some are the result of our own sinful or foolish choices. Sometimes we just don't know any better. Sometimes we're a combination of a lot of things.

Life can be so complicated, and no two stories are exactly alike. Just look at Nicodemus—he was a religious teacher who lived a good life and had a great reputation. He seemed to have it all figured out … until something happened in between.

"I was one way, and now I am completely different. And the thing that happened in between was Him."

There's nothing overly complicated in this statement from Mary to Nicodemus in season 1, episode 2 of **The Chosen**. It was a simple, straightforward explanation of her experience. But it rocked Nicodemus's world.

That's what the gospel—the good news of Jesus Christ—tends to do to people. And Mary's answer sounded a lot like what Jesus explained to Nicodemus in John 3:3: "Truly, truly, I say to you, unless one is born again he cannot see the kingdom of God."

> Figurative language: words or phrases that are meaningful, but not literally true; figures of speech, like metaphors or similes, used to convey a particular idea.

Jesus used figurative language to help Nicodemus understand that before meeting Jesus, he was one way. But after meeting Him, Nicodemus could become someone completely different—he could be born again. He could become someone new.

The idea was staggering and it seemed impossible, especially for an old man like Nicodemus. But being born again just means we go from living one way to living as someone new—which is only possible when something happens in between.

Or, more accurately, Someone.

Mary's and Nico's life stories couldn't have been further apart. Yet their testimonies were ultimately the same: encountering Jesus left them completely different. And encountering Jesus will leave you completely different too.

Because He's the thing that happens in between.

Pray

I was one way and now I am completely different, and the thing that happened in between was You. Thank You for being the **in between**, Jesus. Thank You for not letting me stay stuck in my old ways. You've made me different. You and nothing else. Thank You. Thank You. Thank You.

Reflect

1. Read John 3:1–21. How does knowing more about Nicodemus's story change the way you think about John 3:16 (which is, perhaps, the most famous verse of all time)?

"For God so loved the world, that he gave his only Son, that whoever believes in him should not perish but have eternal life."

John 3:16

2. What is your "one way" story?

3. Have you experienced what Jesus meant when He said you must be born again? If you haven't, try praying this prayer to get your journey with Him started:

Jesus, I know I'm a sinner who needs a Savior. And I know that Savior is You. Please forgive me and come into my life and lead me. I want to be different in the way only You can make me be. Amen.

7

Your True Identity

Some of us long for the days of the dress-up box. That place we went to as a kid where we could pretend to be someone completely different. We'd rummage through to find the perfect princess dress or superhero cape that would complete our outf— well … it's not really an outfit anymore, is it? It's a head-to-toe costume, often including a mask that allows us to assume a completely different identity … usually a persona we think others will like more.

We never really stop playing dress-up. Sometimes it doesn't take much work and we're able to throw on whatever's convenient. In other words, we're comfortable being ourselves. Other times, though, we rummage through everything we've got, looking for the perfect combination. We want to make an impression. We want to be seen by others in a specific way.

We care so very deeply about what others think of us.

In fact, our desire to be accepted goes all the way back to the story of creation in Genesis. When God made Adam, He saw that man was incomplete, so He made Eve. Then we're told that "God saw everything that he had made, and behold, it was very good" (Genesis 1:31).

Unfortunately, it didn't take long for God's very good creation to start playing dress-up. It was actually the first thing Adam and Eve did after introducing sin into the world. They were so worried, so ashamed, about how different they were from each other that they turned fig leaves into the world's first costume—and we've been playing dress up ever since, always trying to cover the things we don't like about ourselves, always trying to be someone different than who we truly are."

And we've been playing dress-up ever since—always trying to cover the things we don't like about ourselves, always trying to be someone different than who we truly are. And in case it isn't obvious yet, we're not talking about actual clothing; we're talking about where we find our identity.

When we met Nicodemus in **The Chosen**, he had the dress-up game nailed. As a prominent Jewish teacher with a large following, Nicodemus wore his Pharisee identity with pride. But when he witnessed Mary Magdalene's complete transformation, it shook his confidence, because who could've performed such an amazing miracle? He was determined to find the answer.

Season 1,
Episode 2

John chapter 3 says: "[Nicodemus] came to Jesus by night and said to him, 'Rabbi, we know that you are a teacher come from God, for no one can do these signs that you do unless God is with him'" (verse 2).

It was great that Nicodemus was asking Jesus questions. But why do you suppose he chose to meet Jesus at night, under the cover of darkness? Perhaps he didn't want anyone to see him, a Pharisee, asking Jesus anything. Perhaps he was protecting his identity as an important

"Now the serpent [i.e., Satan] was more crafty than any other beast of the field that the LORD God had made. He said to the woman, 'Did God actually say, "You shall not eat of any tree in the garden"?'

And the woman said to the serpent, 'We may eat of the fruit of the trees in the garden, but God said, "You shall not eat of the fruit of the tree that is in the midst of the garden, neither shall you touch it, lest you die."'

But the serpent said to the woman, 'You will not surely die. For God knows that when you eat of it your eyes will be opened, and you will be like God, knowing good and evil.'

So when the woman saw that the tree was good for food, and that it was a delight to the eyes, and that the tree was to be desired to make one wise, she took of its fruit and ate, and she also gave some to her husband who was with her, and he ate.

Then the eyes of both were opened, and they knew that they were naked. And they sewed fig leaves together and made themselves loincloths."

Genesis 3:1–7

religious leader. Perhaps, like us, he wasn't quite ready to take off the costume.

John 12:42 actually says, "Many even of the authorities believed in [Jesus], but for fear of the Pharisees they did not confess it, so that they would not be put out of the synagogue."

Perhaps that's why when Jesus invited Nicodemus to follow Him, Nico didn't go. Perhaps he wasn't ready to give up his identity as a Pharisee.

> Pharisees: scholars who interpreted the law to the masses, along with oral traditions. They were connected to the local synagogues and highly respected by the common people.

It would be easy for us to say, "Hey, kid, don't be like Nicodemus." But life is more complicated than that, isn't it? Especially life with Jesus. And the longer we spend playing dress-up with identities that aren't really our own, the harder it is to take off the costumes.

Season 1, Episode 7

But that's the astonishing thing about Jesus. He sees past the things you put on to who you **really** are—and He loves you anyway. He is, in fact, willing to help you through the process of becoming the person He created you to be. He's willing and able to help you find your true identity.

Pray

God, You don't care about the masks I wear or about the costumes I put on. You see through all of it to the real me. Yet I keep going back to the costume box. I'm afraid, Lord. Afraid to take the costume off. Afraid that others will see me and not accept me. God, help me to not be afraid of who YOU made me to be. Help me be the person You want me to be.

Reflect

1. Why do you think Nicodemus had such a hard time giving up his identity as a religious leader?

2. What does your costume look like? What are some of the masks you wear?

3. What does Isaiah 43:1 say about your true identity?

"Fear not, for I have redeemed you; I have called you by name, you are mine."
Isaiah 43:1

A Sound Mind

We're living at a time in history when we hear the words "mental health" on a regular basis, which makes sense because of everything we see happening around us. And **to** us. Depression is on the rise. Eating disorders are on the rise. Crime is on the rise. Fatherlessness, aimlessness, homelessness, hopelessness—all on the rise. Suicide is on the rise.

In light of all that, does anyone know what good mental health actually looks like? As a society, we sure do talk about it a lot. But we're also struggling a whole lot, which begs the question: In such an unhealthy and unstable world, is it possible to have a healthy, stable mind?

That's a big and complex question. But God is big and complex too, and nothing is too difficult for Him to redeem, including and especially the lives of those who look to Him for their identity. For their self-worth. And, yes, for a sound mind.

So, let's start at the start. Because while the world is good at causing and then labeling poor mental health issues, we believe Isaiah 43:1 offers help—a solid foundation for a sound mind.

God says, "Fear not, for I have redeemed you."

Mental health: a person's condition when it comes to their psychological and emotional well-being.

Sound mind: to be reasonable, lucid, and logical.

In the Bible, a sound mind refers not only to understanding right and wrong but being steady enough to choose what's right.

God sees what you're struggling with. He knows you've been hurt. He knows you've hurt yourself and maybe even others by sometimes choosing to sin. He watches you consume the culture along with all its lies and toxicity. He knows the darkness that lives inside your heart (even better than you do)—and He loves you anyway. Not only that, He's moving toward you, offering forgiveness and grace and wholeness and steadiness.

"I have called you by name, you are mine."

God spoke those words to His people, the Israelites, at a time when they were rebelling against Him in every way. But God didn't turn away; instead, He moved toward them and claimed them as His own before they even agreed to be. Their brokenness and instability didn't alter His plans—on the contrary, their value was assigned by the One who knew their names.

Sound familiar?

It should, because the truth is that every follower of Jesus has a not-so-stable "before."

Simon Peter was a rash and reckless fisherman who became a bedrock preacher of the early church, healer of the sick and lame, and fearless unto death.

Nicodemus was a pious, fancy-pants teacher of religion. But he became personal friends with Jesus, finally understanding the Scriptures he'd devoted his life to teaching.

Matthew betrayed his own people by becoming a tax collector for Rome. But he became a member of the elite twelve and author of the first gospel of the New Testament.

Disciples of Jesus are people devoted to following Him, and Jesus had crowds of disciples during His early ministry (and millions of them since!). **Apostles** were the twelve men Jesus chose to be leaders among the rest of His disciples.

Mary of Magdala was possessed by seven demons. Seven! Doesn't get more unstable than that. But she became part of the core group who traveled with Jesus. Not only did she financially support His ministry, she was also the first person He appeared to when He rose from the dead—and then she got to tell the boys.

Here's the point: good mental health begins with knowing Jesus. Period. Jesus is the One who rescues us from darkness and depression and fear. Jesus is the One who never leaves or forsakes us. Jesus is the One who transforms His followers into the people He created them to be. Which means who you see when you look in the mirror doesn't determine **who He sees** or what He will help you become. Nor do your circumstances, other people, or your own choices determine your value; **your value is assigned by the One who knows your name.**

So …

Fear not, God can heal your body, heart, and mind.

Fear not, God can redeem your choices and use them for good.

Fear not, you were made for more than what you've experienced so far.

Fear not, this is only the beginning.

Pray

God, You know me inside and out. You know what I'm struggling with and You also know the way out. Please help me look to You instead of the world around me for stability and for a sound mind. You are steady, Lord. You are solid. You are love and truth and light. I want more of You, Father, and less of me.

Reflect

1. In what ways are you struggling to have a sound mind? Anxiety? Depression? Fear?

2. How does Isaiah 43:1 speak to those things?

3. What do the verses in the margin say about how God sees and helps those who look to Him?

"Trust in the LORD with all your heart, and do not lean on your own understanding. In all your ways acknowledge him, and he will make straight your paths."
Proverbs 3:5–6

*Sometimes the things we struggle with are just too big to deal with on our own. If you're battling any of the things mentioned in this devotional (or something else that wasn't mentioned), please reach out to a trusted adult in your life for help—a parent, a pastor, a Bible study leader, a schoolteacher, a Christian counselor, or a friend.

You don't have to struggle alone.

"The LORD your God is in your midst, a mighty one who will save; he will rejoice over you with gladness; he will quiet you by his love; he will exult over you with loud singing."
Zephaniah 3:17

"Come to me, all who [are weary] and are heavy laden, and I will give you rest. Take my yoke upon you, and learn from me, for I am gentle and lowly in heart, and you will find rest for your souls. For my yoke is easy, and my burden is light."
Matthew 11:28–30

"Cast all your anxieties on [God], because he cares for you."
1 Peter 5:6–7

GUIDED GROUP DISCUSSION

1. It's human nature to long for something more. And it's our human tendency to look for the "more" everywhere other than in God. We look for it in social media likes. We look for it in money. We look for it in relationships. We look for it in our accomplishments. We look for it in our appearance. We look for it in any number of things we don't yet have but imagine would make us happier than we currently are.

And all that longing and looking makes us very **un**happy. Which is why Jesus said, "Everyone who drinks of this water will be thirsty again, but whoever drinks of the water that I will give him **will never be thirsty again**" (John 4:13–14).

In other words, what does God offer that the world just can't provide?

2. Many of us think that in order to have a close relationship with Jesus, we have to be "good" first. But that wasn't true for any of the people we now consider heroes of the faith. Think about it—none of the disciples were perfect people. And their testimonies, while unique, could all be summarized the same way Mary summarized hers in the show:

"I was one way, and now I'm completely different. And the thing that happened in between was Him."

Romans 5:8 says it another way:

"But God shows his love for us in that while we were still sinners, Christ died for us."

In spite of your sin, and in spite of all the things you pursue that **aren't** Him, how does it make you feel to know that Jesus is pursuing you anyway?

3. Jesus doesn't wait for us to be "good." On the contrary, He pursues us while we're still sinners, while we're stuck and broken and in need of what **only He can give.** So, when it comes to our true identity, here's what's actually true:

We are sinners in need of a Savior.

Jesus saves sinners and makes us what we weren't before.

In light of that, what need do we have for the costume box? Hint, hint: we **don't** need it because we've been forgiven and accepted already—which means our true identity is in Jesus. How does knowing that provide stability and security in our very unstable, ever-changing world?

"For all have sinned and fall short of the glory of God."
Romans 3:23

"I have been crucified with Christ. It is no longer I who live, but Christ who lives in me. And the life I now live in the flesh I live by faith in the Son of God, who loved me and gave himself for me."
Galatians 2:20

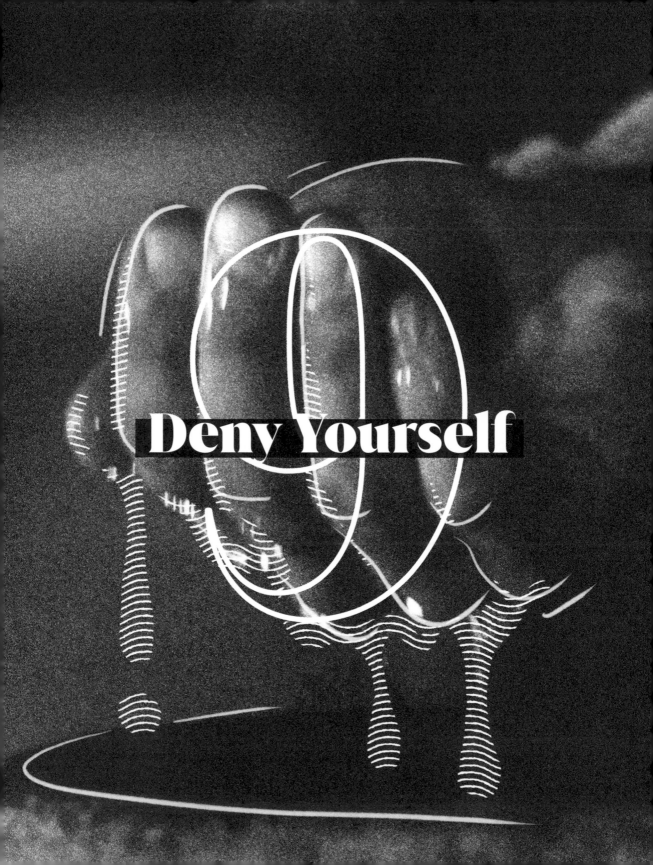

"Then Jesus told his disciples, 'If anyone would come after me, let him deny himself and take up his cross and follow me'" (Matthew 16:24).

Oof. That's a tough little saying from Jesus. There's a lot to unpack in it. He doesn't ease us in; He doesn't mince words. There's no parable with a deeper truth underneath that we have to contemplate and unravel and eventually apply.

Nope, Jesus puts us on blast, plain and simple.

Be honest. It doesn't sound very appealing to deny yourself, does it? If anything, it sounds kind of … awful. Boring, even. Like you have to slog through life with your eyes half-closed. Like you have to say no to everything you might enjoy, everything that smells good, sounds good, tastes good, looks good, or feels good.

Denying yourself definitely doesn't seem like the way to have fun.

But wait. Isn't this the same guy who turned water into wine (gasp) at a wedding feast?

It wasn't that the hosts of the party didn't have any wine at all. They started out with what they thought was plenty. Maybe they didn't plan well enough. Maybe more people showed up than they were expecting. Maybe they accidentally spilled a bunch. Who knows … it doesn't really matter why the wine ran out. The point is that they had some and then they didn't. And in ancient Israel, that would've been a humiliating situation.

Which was why Jesus performed a miracle. And then the party continued.

Season 1,
Episode 5

How do we put those ideas together? How can Jesus be both the life of the party and also the guy telling us to deny ourselves? Well, Jesus helps us understand a little bit more in verses 25–26: "For whoever would save his life will lose it, but whoever loses his life for my sake will find it. For what will it profit a man if he gains the whole world and forfeits his soul?"

Here's the deal. You were created by God, for God. What God wants and what you want aren't supposed to be in competition with each other—they're supposed to be in cooperation.

Here's an example. Let's say you're offered two choices for lunch: your favorite sandwich or a plate of twenty of your favorite sandwiches. Can you eat twenty sandwiches? Um, well, go for it, but you probably won't like the result. Because, as is almost always the case, helping yourself to whatever you want doesn't really help you at all.

Here's the point. Wanting what God wants actually helps you enjoy everything His creation has to offer, because His way is the way that benefits you most!

You follow Jesus because **He knows the way**.

As you follow, you deny yourself because you don't know the way.

That's what it means to take up your cross. Following Jesus costs you everything, but it also gives you everything in return. And the result is ultimately much more enjoyable than going your own way.

Pray

Jesus, You don't always make sense to me. I'm just being honest. You turn water into wine. But You also tell me to deny myself. I know that following You will cost me everything, but I also know You want to give me everything in return. Help me, Jesus, understand the difference between enjoying my favorite sandwich and eating twenty of them.

Reflect

1. What's your favorite thing to eat for lunch? Seriously, write it down. Now, what would happen if you ate twenty of them? Seriously, write it down.

2. OK, let's stick with the metaphor a bit longer. What are your "twenty sandwiches" in real life? Meaning, what are the things God made for your enjoyment, but you have a hard time not overindulging?

> Overindulging = too much

3. What do you think it means that what God wants and what you want don't have to be in competition with each other? What do you think it means to deny yourself when they **do** compete?

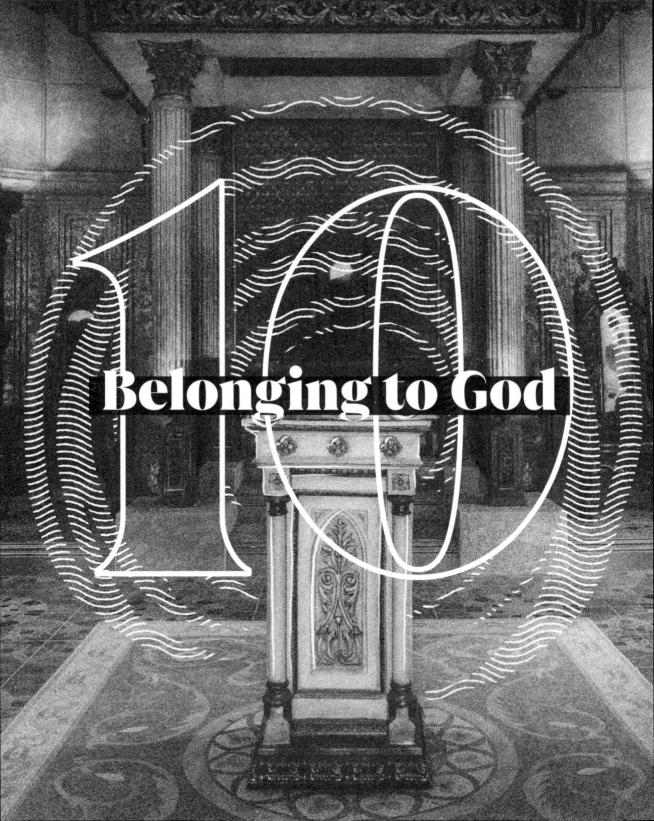

10

Belonging to God

What does it mean to belong to God? Honestly, the whole idea sounds a little weird, doesn't it? Especially to our twenty-first-century ears. Humans have lived in self-centered mode since way back in the Garden of Eden, when Adam and Eve listened to the serpent and ate the fruit of the forbidden tree (Genesis 3).

They were thinking of themselves.

Things haven't changed much since then. Except now, even the technology that's supposed to make life easier (especially your phone) reinforces the idea that you belong to YOU. That life is about seeing and doing and being **what** you want, **when** you want it, **how** you want it.

But what does it mean to belong to God instead? Well, let's start with what belonging to God **doesn't** mean. It doesn't mean you become a religious robot, devoid of personality. And it doesn't mean you become a religious puppet with some heavenly force pulling your strings.

Ironically, **belonging to God does mean you've been set free.** When Jesus tried to help the disciples understand this idea, He said it this way: "You will know the truth, and the truth will set you **free**" (John 8:32). Which actually means you're free from being a robot who mindlessly follows others. You're free from being a puppet controlled by your self-focused drives and desires.

You're free from being enslaved by sin (verse 34).

When the Bible says, "I have called you by name, **you are mine**" (Isaiah 43:1), what are you actually supposed to do with that? Well, clearly Jesus doesn't just show up, give you a hug, and then leave you alone. Just as He did for Mary of Magdala and the rest of the disciples, He's inviting you into a way of life, a way of learning how to live with Him at the center instead of you.

And it starts with admitting a couple of things: (1) your self-centered life is a dead end because living without God doesn't get you where you truly want to go, and (2) you were created to belong to and be in relationship with God.

Season 1,
Episode 6

Of course, these admissions aren't a magic wand that fixes everything that's broken. Life, as you already know, is way messier than that. Changing your mind and heart from being self-focused to being God-focused (i.e., believing you belong to Him instead of yourself) takes time. In fact, throughout the New Testament we see that even the disciples didn't get it right away—and they had Jesus right in front of them! They didn't automatically figure it all out when they started following Him.

Neither will you. But life change begins with knowing who you belong to … and that He loves you enough to call you His own.

Pray

Lord, I'm so tired of belonging to myself—it's not working. I want to belong to You, but I don't always know how. Help me see things differently. Help me let go of my self-centered ways and to be set free from sin. Thank You for loving me and calling me by name.

> "Thus says the LORD, he who created you … he who formed you: 'Fear not, for I have redeemed you; I have called you by name. YOU. ARE. MINE.'"
> Isaiah 43:1

Reflect

1. In what ways are you self-focused?

2. What does it mean to be a robot who mindlessly follows others? To be a puppet who's controlled by self-focused drives and desires (sin)?

3. What does it mean to be set free from sin? How would it feel to fully belong to God instead?

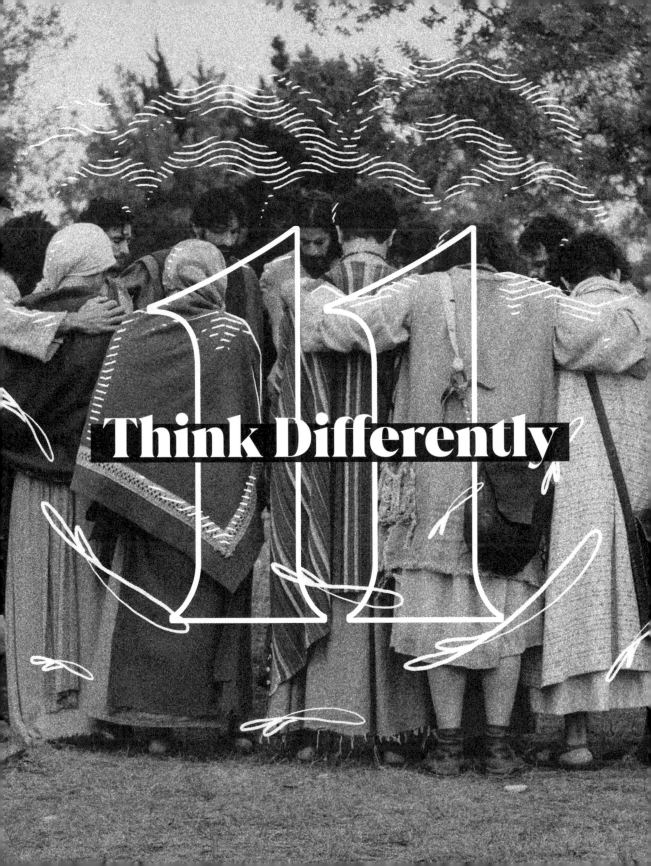

Think Differently

Jesus collected a crazy group of followers, didn't He? Individually, choosing them sort of made sense. A group of fishermen would've been able to roll up their sleeves, catch dinner, and make camp. A tax collector could've been the brains of the operation. And you wouldn't have to worry about thugs or thieves with a trained Zealot on the squad.

But combined they looked more like misfits. Oddballs. Weirdos, even. Especially when you include the women (check out Luke 8). Because in first-century Israel, it would've been downright scandalous for unmarried women to travel with men they weren't related to.

Plus, the disciples didn't always get along, which made the group dynamic even stranger. Luke 22:24 gives us this insight from the Last Supper: "A dispute also arose among them, as to which of them was to be regarded as the greatest." In other words, on the final night of Jesus's life, His closest friends were arguing over who was the best—and the category wasn't "most humble."

But, despite appearances, Jesus was intentional about who He chose. And **how many** He chose. Because the twelve disciples corresponded with the twelve ancient tribes of Israel, ten of which had been lost over the course of a few hundred years due to warring and enslavement and all manner of trouble.

By the time Jesus arrived, the Jews had been living under oppressive Roman rule and they were longing for rescue. They were waiting and watching for the prophesied Messiah, the One they believed would overthrow the occupation, restore the twelve tribes, and reestablish them in their homeland.

In other words, this seemingly random group of Jesus-following misfits became the foundation of a movement that would change the world.

Which brings us to you.

If you are part of a youth group, think about them for a moment. Chances are, you didn't pick them. Maybe a parent dragged you to church. Maybe a friend invited you to come and see. However you got there, you'd likely be OK if a few people stopped coming. Thing is, we're drawn to those who are like us in some way: what we listen to, how we look, what we watch, what we eat, what we won't eat, how we dress, who we cheer for, who we don't like, what we play, where we're from.

There's nothing inherently wrong with forming friendships based on the things we have in common. We were created to be social, to want to belong, and to live in community with others. But all of that makes the **differences** between Jesus's first followers so important.

Remember when Matthew was called in **The Chosen**? Simon didn't want it to happen, and his conversation with Jesus went like this:

Season 1,
Episode 7

"Do you have any idea what this guy has done? I don't get it."
"You didn't get it when I chose you, either."
"But this is different!"
"Get used to different."

Turns out, Jesus had something incredibly special in store for His oddballs. He didn't select them based on what everyone else could see. He chose them based on who He knew they'd become. Shortly after gathering them together, He sent them out "to proclaim the kingdom of God and to heal" (Luke 9:2). They were chosen by Him to build His kingdom.

Now, back to your youth group. What if (and this is a crazy idea) Jesus has brought your group together too? What if, like the disciples, He has something special in store for each of you there? It probably won't be easy—group projects never are. It might even feel a little bit … different.

But maybe—just maybe—He wants you to get used to different.

Pray

Jesus, help me embrace the people You've put in my life, especially the ones I didn't choose. Help me see people differently, including in my youth group. Honestly, sometimes I wish some of them weren't there. I need Your help, Jesus, to see them the way You do. And we all need Your help to see what You have in store for us. Help me get used to different.

Reflect

1. When it comes to Jesus's followers, do any of His choices surprise you? Why, or why not?

If you're not currently in a youth group, try to find one in your area. The Bible tells us again and again to be in a community of believers so that we don't have to follow Jesus alone! And so we experience Him moving in and among His people. "For where two or three are gathered in my name, there am I among them." Matthew 18:20

2. Is there someone in your youth group you need to start seeing differently?

3. What special purpose do you think Jesus might have in bringing the people in your church or prayer group at school together?

12

Jesus-Centered

We're going to take a detour in today's devotional by starting in outer space before orbiting our way back to the Bible. And our little jaunt has **everything** to do with your identity.

Let's start with a pop quiz: The giant rock you live on (aka, Earth) revolves around something—what is that something called?

Hint: it's at the center of our solar system.

Hint, hint: it rhymes with **fun**.

OK, so maybe that wasn't the hardest test you'll ever take. If you didn't get it after the second clue, we might need to have a chat. Either way, you don't have to be an astronomer or have a telescope to know the earth revolves around the **sun**.

But here's a crazy fact. For the majority of the world's history, people believed the sun revolved around the earth, not the other way around. From their perspective, the earth was the center of the universe.

It wasn't until around five hundred years ago that a scientist named Copernicus kicked down the door on that way of thinking. And it wasn't a little kick, either. It was more like a pro-wrestler-style running dropkick (minus all the yelling and tights). In fact, the change in perspective rocked people's worldview so much, it became known as the "Copernican Revolution."

Because it was revolutionary.

Of course, people didn't like finding out that they, along with the sun, weren't the center of the universe. So, despite the overwhelming evidence, it took another 150 years for full acceptance to take hold.

Here's what we're getting at. Every day you're told that **you** are the center of your universe. (Remember the hamster wheel?) But what you need—what we all need—is a revolutionary change in perspective.

When Jesus shows up, He takes the idea that everything revolves around you and dropkicks it into the next galaxy. And, boy, does it hurt. Giving up something you assumed was true for a long time **takes** time. It isn't easy. Redefining yourself from the center of the universe to the one who orbits around the Son also isn't easy. (See what we did there?)

Maybe that's why it took Simon so long to believe the Savior, the true center of the universe, had finally arrived. Prior to Jesus's arrival, he spent so much time trying to save himself. And maybe that's why Nicodemus had such a hard time changing his perspective. For decades he studied and taught the old way of thinking. And maybe that's why Mary Magdalene was so scared, and why she momentarily tried to run away from Jesus. She just couldn't imagine there being a different way to live.

And maybe that's why you sometimes resist Jesus too, because changing your perspective is hard. It might even make you feel like you're losing something. But if you want to start looking toward the **actual** center of the universe, if you want to start basing your identity on what's true, **you're gonna need a Jesus revolution.**

Pray

God, You are the center of the universe. I want You to also be the center of **my** universe. You don't change, and You're always right there. But I'm not always looking in the right direction. And I'm not quite sure I'm ready. Honestly, sometimes I just don't want to change what I'm thinking or doing. Help me, Jesus, to change my perspective. Help me see You, right where You've always been.

Reflect

1. What is the danger of having a self-centered perspective?

2. Why do you think it's so hard to have a Jesus-centered perspective?

3. Take some time to read Philippians 2:1–11. How might this passage lead to a Jesus revolution in your own heart?

GUIDED GROUP DISCUSSION

1. To find ourselves we must deny ourselves. Wait—what? How does that make any sense? Well, as we've been discussing, we're **following** Jesus, which means He's leading and we're not.

Duh. (Again.)

What does it mean to follow Jesus by denying yourself?

> "Then Jesus told his disciples, 'If anyone would come after me, let him deny himself and take up his cross and follow me.'"
> Matthew 16:24

2. Our culture constantly preaches that you belong to you. That life is about being free to see and do and be whatever you want, whenever you want it, and however you want it.

But is that true? Does doing what you want and making everything about yourself **actually** satisfy your deepest longings to be loved and accepted? To belong? To be free?

What actually makes us free? Who actually satisfies us?

> "So Jesus said to [His followers], 'If you abide
> in my word, you are truly my disciples, and
> you will know the truth, and the truth will set
> you free.… Truly, truly, I say to you, everyone
> who practices sin is a slave to sin.… [But] if the
> Son sets you free, you will be free indeed.'"
> John 8:31–36

3. Nowadays it's a revolutionary thought that we **aren't** the center of the universe. That everything isn't supposed to be about "self," but instead everything is about Jesus. What He did for us, how He loves us, and what He wants to do in our lives.

To that end, read Philippians 2:1–11 out loud together:

"So if there is any encouragement in Christ, any
comfort from love, any participation in the Spirit,
any affection and sympathy, complete my joy by
being of the same mind, having the same love,
being in full accord and of one mind. Do nothing
from selfish ambition or conceit, but in humility
count others more significant than yourselves.

Let each of you look not only to his own
interests, but also to the interests of others.

Have this mind among yourselves, which is
yours in Christ Jesus, who, though he was in the
form of God, did not count equality with God
a thing to be grasped, but emptied himself, by
taking the form of a servant, being born in the
likeness of men. And being found in human form,
he humbled himself by becoming obedient to
the point of death, even death on a cross.

Therefore God has highly exalted him and
bestowed on him the name that is above
every name, **so that at the name of
Jesus every knee should bow,**
in heaven and on earth and under the earth,
and every tongue confess that Jesus Christ
is Lord, to the glory of God the Father."

Part 2

Learning to Follow Jesus

13

A Different Kind of Kingdom

In the final episode of season 2, just before Jesus went to preach the Sermon on the Mount, Matthew offered Him some honest feedback: "Do you realize how heavy laden your sermon is with these kinds of ominous pronouncements?" Jesus calmly responded, "It's a manifesto, Matthew. I'm not here to be sentimental and soothing. I'm here to start a revolution."

Well, **that's** different. Nowadays, a lot of people think Jesus was a nice guy who said nice things about loving our enemies and giving to the poor. And, of course, He is loving and He offers salvation to anyone and everyone who believes that He's God's Son, the Savior of the world (John 3:16–18).

But have you ever considered that He started a revolution?

Put yourself in the Jewish people's shoes for a minute. Your country has been invaded multiple times, and your conquerors (like Quintus) rule over you with a heavy hand. An occupying nation oppresses your beliefs, mistreats your neighbors, and imposes crippling taxes. Your people have been waiting for hundreds of years for an

Season 2,
Episode 8

Ominous:
giving the impression
that something bad is
going to happen.

Pronouncement:
an announcement.
Which means Matthew was
concerned that Jesus's words
would turn people away.

Manifesto:
a public declaration
of policy or goals.

Revolution:
an overthrow of a
government or social order
in favor of a new system.

organized revolt and the freedom it would bring. In fact, prophets like Isaiah have actually promised God would send a new king who would establish an entirely new kingdom.

Which means you don't just dream of revolution—you ache for it.

Then Jesus shows up and you think maybe He could be the Anointed One, the Messiah. So, you follow the crowds to the mountainside, expecting to hear Him preach about fighting back against Rome. But instead, He says crazy things like "Love your enemies and pray for those who persecute you" (Matthew 5:44).

Wait, what? No way. That wouldn't sound like the uprising everyone's been waiting for. And in the show, Matthew had the same reaction, to which Jesus clarified: "I said **revolution**, not a revolt. I'm talking about a radical shift."

Indeed, Jesus came to establish the new kingdom the nation of Israel was longing for.

But not the one they were expecting.

People do indeed sometimes reduce Jesus's message to a nice, manageable checklist that goes something like this: pray a prayer, get saved, go to church, go to heaven.

But life in Jesus's kingdom is so much more. **So. Much. More.**

Following Jesus cannot be reduced to a simple checklist. In fact, it includes being willing to do things that are new, even contrary to what you were expecting—like loving your enemies and praying for those who persecute you. And Jesus never said to just pray a prayer, get saved, and then keep living the way you had been before you met Him.

Instead, He says, "Follow Me."

Follow Me and you'll experience a life worth living. Follow Me and I'll show you the beauty of turning the other cheek. Follow Me and you'll see the power of forgiving those who've wronged you. Follow

Me and you'll know the peace of giving and receiving unconditional love. Follow Me and you'll gain strength that comes from surrender. Follow Me and you'll have joy in the midst of suffering.

This is what life is like in Jesus's kingdom.

And it's revolutionary.

Pray

Jesus, I desperately want to follow You and be part of Your kingdom. Help me join Your revolution, here and now. I admit that change is scary and is sometimes really hard. But, deep down, I know living in Your kingdom is the life I've always wanted. Help me live in it today.

Reflect

1. What are some things you've heard or assumed it means to follow Jesus?

2. Read 1 Peter 2:9–25 (it's a doozy!). What does Peter say it actually means to follow Jesus?

3. Matthew 4:17 says, "Jesus began to preach, saying, 'Repent, for the kingdom of heaven is at hand.'" In other words, confess and turn away from your sin so that you can join the revolution! Jesus's ministry—His heavenly kingdom—has come to earth. The question is, do you want to be part of it?

Apprentice

When Jesus says "Follow Me," it's not about following Him to heaven—at least, not yet. It's about living life in a way that allows you to see heaven here and now: "Repent, for the kingdom of heaven is at hand" (Matthew 4:17).

It's about living a life of purpose: "Follow me, and I will make you fishers of men" (Matthew 4:19).

It's about living a life of meaning: "I chose you … that you should go and bear fruit and that your fruit should abide … These things I command you, so that you will love one another" (John 15:16–17).

It's about living a life that moves you from darkness to light: "Jesus spoke to them, saying, 'I am the light of the world. Whoever follows me will not walk in darkness, but will have the light of life'" (John 8:12).

It's about living life as Jesus's apprentice.

Season 2, Episode 8

The Sermon on the Mount turned the world upside down, and the revolution Jesus preached has continued for two thousand years—because Jesus's teachings show us how to choose a different kind of life. Different at home and at school. Different in our relationships and rivalries. Different in our fears and hopes and hurts and dreams.

No doubt, the disciples began to experience those differences, not by following Jesus for a day or two, but by choosing to follow Him in everything for the rest of their lives. That said, there's nothing magical about the word **disciple** (even though when we consider the

heroes of the Christian faith, we often give that word extra weight and clout). When people in the first century heard that title, they would picture a student or—more accurately—an apprentice.

The dictionary defines an apprentice as one who is learning a trade, art, or calling through practical experience under a skilled worker.

Jesus is the skilled worker, and He wants to teach you the art of living in the world. And if finding your identity in Jesus is the way off the hamster wheel of self-centeredness, living as His apprentice is the way to keep you from getting back on. It helps you walk, **not in darkness**, but alongside the light of life.

So, how can you get your apprenticeship started?

Here are three simple things you can do:

Be patient with yourself, because Jesus is. It's OK to ask Him for help. You can't be His apprentice in your own strength—that's the whole point. It's easy to get discouraged and let a mistake or outright failure knock you off course. So, be honest with Jesus in prayer when it happens. He'll be right there to pick you up and help you get going again.

> Disciple =
> Apprentice =
> Jesus Follower

Practice. Think about your favorite pro athlete or band. Chances are they didn't wake up one morning with the ability to throw a perfect curveball or play a killer riff. In our next devotion, we'll start looking at some of the spiritual exercises that'll help you train so you can live the kind of life Jesus lived. In other words, you're gonna need to practice.

Choose. Most of us want what's best, at least in theory. But there's a distinct difference between **wanting** and **doing**. In fact, we actually waste a lot of time trying to avoid the kind of life we know is best. It takes conscious choices every day to follow Jesus and His way of life—which means living as His apprentice starts with choosing to do so.

Are you ready to choose?

Pray

Jesus, thank You for showing me how to live. Thank You for providing ways to stay on the path to God and away from sin. Thank You for choosing me as Your apprentice and for teaching me through Your words and Your life how to follow. Thank You for not only offering me an eternity spent with You, but also a life lived—here and now—with You.

Reflect

1. What does the word **apprentice** mean to you?

2. Why is it important to think of yourself as Jesus's apprentice, and how might that change your life?

3. Are you ready to choose to live a life of apprenticeship? Why, or why not?

15
Spiritual Training

Before you start today's devotional, here's a quick challenge for you: go run a marathon. It'll probably take you awhile, but it's not a big deal—just a mere twenty-six miles.

OK, maybe running's not your thing, so here's a different idea: play the national anthem on an instrument you've never even picked up before.

Obviously, we're joking because you'd never show up expecting to win the Boston Marathon without training first, nor would you become a violinist in the Chicago Symphony Orchestra on day one of playing. Nope. The people who participate in those things **prepare**. Violinists practice for hours on end. Marathon runners train every day. Ultimately, they build their lives around acquiring the skills they need to perform when the time comes.

When we're introduced to Simon "Z" in season 2, we see him training as a Zealot. History teaches that the Zealots took their religious beliefs to the extreme, actively inciting violence against their Roman rulers. But after his brother Jesse was healed, Z was ready to follow Jesus to the ends of the earth: "I've been training my whole life for this," Z told Jesus. "I am ready to execute Your mission today."

Season 2,
Episode 5

"We'll see," Jesus replied. "Show Me your weapon."

And then He chucked Z's dagger into the water.

It was a hard lesson for a Zealot to learn. The revolution Jesus was ushering in was a spiritual one. It had nothing to do with overthrowing

Rome; rather, it was about overthrowing the forces of evil that prevent us from living in God's spiritual kingdom.

Here's how the apostle Paul explained it in a letter to his apprentice, Timothy:

"Have nothing to do with irreverent, silly myths. Rather train yourself for godliness; for while bodily training is of some value, godliness is of value in every way, as it holds promise for the present life and also for the life to come."

1 Timothy 4:7–8

If finding our identity in Jesus is the way off the hamster wheel of self-centeredness, spiritual training keeps us from climbing back on it. The godliness that results holds promises for your life right now! But becoming—and remaining—Jesus's apprentice requires we actively train to be more like Him.

This is where this devotional book you're holding gets really real: **We become more like Jesus by doing what He did.**

To be clear, we're not encouraging you to drop out of school and go camping in the wilderness for forty days (although Jesus did in Matthew 4:1–11). While time away from school might sound nice, that's probably not going to convince the adults in your life. But you can adopt a spiritual training program similar to Jesus's by spending time with God, talking to Him in prayer and reading your Bible, and by serving others.

Spiritual exercise can also be something simple like choosing to sit by the kid no one else wants to sit with—**because that's the kind of thing Jesus would do.**

Over the next few weeks, we'll introduce you to different spiritual exercises. We encourage you to try each one, no matter how challenging (or strange) they seem. As a result, you'll see two things happen: First, you'll grow more connected to God. This connection is what enabled Jesus to perform well in the moments that mattered, and it will do the same for you. Second, it will help you lay aside the "sin which clings so closely" (Hebrews 12:1), which will keep you off that stupid hamster wheel.

You can do this. So let's get started.

Pray

Jesus, I'm beginning to understand more about what it means to be Your apprentice. As I continue my journey of following You, please help me figure out what my spiritual training program should look like. To be honest, I'm a bit overwhelmed just thinking about it. So, help me keep it simple and to take life one day (and one exercise) at a time.

Reflect

1. Why is an intentional spiritual training program important?

2. Like Z, what "dagger" will you need to throw away in order to begin training? In other words, what or who (**other than Jesus**) are you placing your self-worth, sense of security, or hope in?

3. Read 1 Timothy 4:7–8 in the margin. What areas of your life will benefit from greater spiritual training?

> "Train yourself for godliness; for while bodily training is of some value, godliness is of value in every way, as it holds promise for the present life and also for the life to come."
>
> 1 Timothy 4:7–8

10
Spending Time in Prayer (Part 1)

In **The Chosen**, we see Jesus and His followers regularly engaging in prayer. One of these prayers is the "Shema" and it goes like this: "Hear O Israel, the Lord is our God, the Lord is One."

Season 2, Episode 1

Near the end of one of the episodes, Big James and John enjoyed a special moment with Jesus. After they woke up, they realized that Melech (the owner of the field they had plowed) had been healed. Then, together, they said the "Modeh Ani" prayer with Jesus: "I am thankful before You, living and enduring King, for You have mercifully restored my soul within me. Great is Your faithfulness …"

There are two things to note about these prayers. First, they were (and still are) a normal part of daily Jewish life. Second, the last thing Jesus did before sleeping was pray, and the first thing He did upon waking was pray.

Clearly, prayer is an important part of being an apprentice to Jesus. In fact, in His famous Sermon on the Mount, Jesus taught His followers another prayer, often referred to as "The Lord's Prayer." So, let's do exactly what Jesus told His followers (which includes us) to do.

In Hebrew, the word **shema** means "to hear," but it also implies the effect of hearing. In other words, to hear and to listen, to take heed, to be obedient, and to do what is being asked.

Modeh Ani: pronounced moe-de-ah-nee. In Hebrew, these words mean "to admit, to thank, and to surrender." In this morning prayer, the Jews acknowledge God's gifts and their dependence on/ need for Him.

"And when you pray, you must not be like the hypocrites. For they love to stand and pray in the synagogues and at the street corners, that they may be seen by others. Truly, I say to you, they have received their reward. But when you pray, go into your room and shut the door and pray to your Father who is in secret. And your Father who sees in secret will reward you.

And when you pray, do not heap up empty phrases as the Gentiles do, for they think that they will be heard for their many words. Do not be like them, for your Father knows what you need before you ask him.

Pray then like this:

Our Father in heaven, hallowed be your name. Your kingdom come, your will be done, on earth as it is in heaven.

As you pray, think about what the words mean:

Our Father in heaven

(Acknowledge that God is over everything)

Hallowed be your name

(Agree that God's name is to be revered and honored)

Your kingdom come, your will be done

(Call on God to do what He wants, not what you want)

Give us this day our daily bread

(Ask God for what you need)

And forgive our debts

(Repent of any sin in your life)

As we also have forgiven

(Forgive others)

And lead us not into temptation, but deliver us from evil

(Ask for help to resist sin)

Give us this day our daily bread, and forgive us our debts, as we also have forgiven our debtors. And lead us not into temptation, but deliver us from evil.

For if you forgive others their trespasses, your heavenly Father will also forgive you."
Matthew 6:5–14

We'll look at another prayer next week. But for now, practice this simple spiritual exercise: for the next week, either when you wake up or just before you go to bed, **pray the Lord's Prayer.**

That's all. Seven days, a few short moments per day.

You'll likely find it gets easier each time, and you might even have this specific prayer memorized by the end of the week. Perhaps it'll lead you into deeper conversations with God as you go. Either way, you'll stretch those spiritual muscles as you continue your apprenticeship with Jesus.

Pray

You got this one. ☺

Reflect

1. What's significant about the Jewish people praying first thing in the morning and last thing in the evening?

2. Why do you think it's important to often pray, as Jesus instructed, in secret?

3. What time of day will you commit to praying the Lord's Prayer for the next week?

GUIDED GROUP DISCUSSION

Jesus was not the conquering hero the Jews were expecting the Messiah to be. They were waiting and watching for the One who would rescue them from Rome by way of military might.

But Jesus said, "Love your enemies and pray for those who persecute you" (Matthew 5:44).

To be clear, Jesus **is** the conquering hero because He defeated sin and death on the cross. He made a way for us to be forgiven and restored to a right relationship with God. He made it possible for us to be His apprentices.

1. How is Jesus different than you expected?

2. What does it mean to be Jesus's apprentice, and how might accepting the position change your life?

3. Why do you suppose praying was one of the first things Jesus taught His disciples to do, and how would more time spent talking to God change the way you live each day?

Spending Time in God's Word (Part 1)

The first episode of season 2 opened with a surprise. A much older John sat in a room listening to his much older friends share their stories about Jesus. And he wrote everything down in what would become the Gospel of John in the New Testament.

Season 2, Episode 1

Think about that for a moment: the Gospel of John is an eyewitness account of Jesus's life and teachings. Which means you can hold in your hands words that were written by someone who actually saw Jesus with his own eyeballs.

It's easy to take that for granted, and to miss the significance of being able to read firsthand accounts of Jesus. It's also easy to take our **access** to the Bible for granted.

In Jesus's day, Old Testament Scripture was kept in synagogues. Not in homes. Not on shelves or in desk drawers. Not on phones kept in pockets. Instead, Scripture was recorded on scrolls, and those scrolls were kept in special rooms only a few had access to. So, people would gather in their places of worship to hear Scripture read aloud by religious leaders.

> Access:
> our permission or ability
> to approach or enter
> a place; to obtain,
> examine, or retrieve.

The people didn't otherwise have access to the Word of God.

Fast-forward to the 1450s when the printing press revolutionized the availability of Scripture, making it easier and more affordable for people to own and share the Bible. The revolution continued with the introduction of mass communication in the twentieth century (think: radio and television). And now, the internet and smartphones make it **even** easier and **even** more affordable to read the Bible than at any other point in history.

That's a good thing. But like we said, we take it for granted. Which means today's spiritual exercise is an important one. As you read the Lord's Prayer, add one thing to the beginning:

ask God to reveal Himself to you in His Word.

That's it. Nothing fancy, nothing complicated. Just something to remind you that (a) you have direct access to God through Scripture (amazing!), and (b) you get to experience and encounter the same Jesus that John saw with his own eyeballs.

Pray

Father, please reveal Yourself to me in Your Word.

Reflect

1. How does technology both help and hurt the way you read and interact with the Bible?

2. How does the idea of experiencing Jesus in the Bible change the way you read it?

3. Why do you think developing a regular exercise of Bible reading is important?

18

Surrender

What do you dream about? We're not talking about the ones you have while you're snoring. We're talking about the big dreams, the what-you-wanna-be-when-you-grow-up kind of dreams. The ones you have **before** you fall asleep, when you're lying in bed thinking about who you want to become, the things you want to do in this life, and maybe even the person you want to spend it with.

Those dreams tell us a lot about ourselves. It's not so much **what** we dream about that gives us insight; it's what those dreams reveal about our motivations—about what we truly care about. We dream about being important, sounding smart, and being beautiful. We dream about being like other people and maybe a little less weird. We dream about making a difference, about doing something significant in the world. We dream about being loved or maybe just being liked.

When we were introduced to Nathanael in **The Chosen**, we saw his dreams come crashing down around him. Literally. In the show's depiction, he was an architect who worked his way up because he wanted to build great things for God. But then, just like that, his entire career—everything he'd worked for—was reduced to rubble.

Season 2,
Episode 2

Under the fig tree, Nathanael had that terrible, all-too-familiar feeling ... you know the one. That hurt and pain you feel when things don't go the way you wanted them to. When what you care about so deeply ends up in pieces, and you're left wondering what happened and where you went wrong. Perhaps you even wonder why God failed you and if He cares about you at all.

Truth is, Nathanael had been running on his own hamster wheel of hubris (as he told the bartender), which is a fancy word for "pride." Of course, his pride didn't get him where he wanted to go—the hamster wheel never does. But then Philip invited him to come and see Jesus. And then Jesus invited him to follow.

Jesus didn't just want His new recruit to travel with Him around the countryside. Accepting the Lord's invitation meant Nathanael would have to give up his own plans and dreams. He would have to turn over his deep-seated desires, along with his beliefs about what would make him happy.

Nathanael had to surrender.

Ironically, when he did, he found the same freedom God offers you. Freedom from the relentless drive to have everything go your own way. Freedom from needing the approval of others. Freedom from insatiable desires like pride, greed, vanity, and lust. Freedom from your self-centered nature and the sin it breeds in your life.

When we choose to surrender, we're in good company because Jesus lived His entire life with that same attitude: "[Jesus] did not count equality with God something to be grasped, but emptied himself, by taking the form of a bondservant … He humbled himself by becoming obedient to the point of death: death on the cross" (Philippians 2:6–8).

Jesus was fully surrendered.

> **Insatiable:**
> having an appetite or desire that is impossible to satisfy.

> **Bondservant:**
> a slave.
>
> In Roman times, the term **bondservant** could refer to someone who voluntary served as a slave, but typically referred to one in a permanent position of serving. Jesus "took the form of a bondservant" when He chose to become a man … and then He served to the point of death.

And He's the One we follow.

Today's spiritual exercise will help you take baby steps down the path of following Jesus into a life of surrender. What you'll do is super simple and only takes a few seconds. But there's a catch because simple doesn't mean easy … surrendering never is.

Nevertheless, sit up and place your hands on your knees. Make fists with your hands. Now, close your eyes (well, you might want to finish reading this first) and take a deep breath. As you exhale, turn your fists over and open them. Then say this line from the Lord's Prayer:

Your kingdom come, Your will be done, on earth as it is in heaven.

There's nothing magical about those words, and they won't automatically change your desires. But you're learning to turn things over to God. You're posturing yourself on the outside in the same way you'll need to posture your heart. Because following Jesus means you'll have to entrust your dreams to Him.

> The posture of your heart = your approach to and your attitude before God.

So, pray this prayer as you unball your fists and begin the process of surrender.

Pray

Father, I'm hanging on to my dreams so tightly. There are some things, even now, that I don't really want to surrender to You. Help me learn to let go. Your kingdom come, Your will be done, on earth as it is in heaven. Give me the strength to mean it, Lord.

Reflect

1. What do you think it means that even though He was God, Jesus didn't consider equality with God something to be grasped (i.e., held on to)?

2. What is one thing you're grasping too tightly? It could be thoughts, a grudge, your goals, or an emotion.

3. How would an attitude of surrender affect your life? How might it bring you **more** freedom, not less, as the world would have you believe?

Worship 10

When Nathanael sat under the fig tree and lit his architectural drawings on fire, he did something we might expect in that moment: he wept and mourned the loss of his dream. But then, he looked toward heaven and started doing something … **un**expected: he worshipped God, even as his dreams were turning to ash.

"Blessed are You, Lord our God, King of the universe. Hear O Israel, the Lord our God, the Lord is One."

That isn't what typically comes to mind when we think about worshipping, is it? Usually there's a bunch of people in a room together, all singing the same song. And while that's certainly a common way to worship, it isn't the only way.

Season 2, Episode 2

Worship puts God where He belongs— at the center of your attention. When Nathanael said, "The Lord is One," he was reminding himself of who God is. He was posturing his heart and mind in reverence. He was redirecting his focus back to God and praising in spite of his grief—because that's what God deserves.

Worship moves us to confession—because focusing on God helps us see who we really are. It reveals our motivation and exposes our hearts … which means it helps us deal more honestly with God … which means our worship isn't always controlled or contained or even pretty.

In the ancient world, most religions worshipped many gods and goddesses, which made the Hebrew faith and their worship of only one God very unique. "The Lord is One" is the opening line in the Shema prayer, and a declaration of that truth.

Under the fig tree, Nathanael's praise led to this honest and messy plea: "Do not hide Your face from me. Do You see me …? Do You see me?" He was raw and real and wounded and needy; worship has a way of bringing those things to the surface. But it also has a way of reminding us that God is bigger than our problems, and that He welcomes us, just as we are.

And so, **worship draws us close to the One who cares for us most,** which makes it an incredibly important spiritual exercise, whether it takes place with a group of people or when you're alone in your room. It doesn't have to be complicated or organized; simple statements like the one from the Lord's Prayer are worship:

"Our Father in heaven, hallowed be Your name."

When you shift your focus from yourself to God, you're climbing off that exhausting hamster wheel of self-worth and self-help and self-medication. You're declaring God **and God alone** deserves to be at the center of your life. You're confessing His worthiness to be praised in spite of hard circumstances. You're admitting your inability to navigate hard things without His help.

Worship doesn't require a song, though you're welcome to sing. It doesn't demand a psalm, though Scripture is full of words we sometimes don't have. Bottom line: your worship doesn't have to be anything other than simply turning your heart toward heaven and declaring:

"You are God and I am not."

Pray

You are God and I am not. You are the One who created the universe, who created everything, who created me—and I am not. You are the One who holds the entire world together—and I am not. You, heavenly Father, are high above it all. Help me turn my heart toward You today.

Reflect

1. Why do we sometimes forget who God is? How does worship help us remember?

2. What is one thing you can do to worship God today?

3. What does worshipping God reveal to you about yourself? Is there something you need to confess in order to make God the center of your life?

Service

Focusing on others is the easiest way to not focus on yourself. Well, duh.

That's an obvious statement. But, man, it's hard to do and even the disciples didn't get it right. In season 2, episode 3, we watched them struggle to understand this part of Jesus's teaching and ministry. What began as a discussion about the incredible things they were witnessing turned into an argument about what Jesus would do next. Later, a simple conversation about the day took a hard turn toward Matthew's past as a tax collector, and it ended in an eruption of anger from Simon; he swore he'd never forgive Matthew.

But at that moment, Jesus returned to camp, filthy and moving slowly because He was exhausted from a day spent healing people.

Season 2,
Episode 3

"Good night," He said, stumbling toward His tent.

It's a pretty incredible picture, isn't it? Jesus's followers fighting one another while He was out serving others. It was something He had to teach them about constantly, all the way up to the week before His death. Even then, they tried to elbow past each other for power, asking Jesus for important roles in His kingdom. But Jesus patiently tried to help them see that His kingdom wasn't about overthrowing Romans—or each other: "But whoever would be great among you must be your servant … the Son of Man came not to be served but to serve" (Matthew 20:26–28).

To make it even simpler, Jesus said, "The last will be first, and the first last" (20:16). But they still didn't get it. So, on the night before He died, Jesus gave a powerful visual reminder of His upside-down, last-is-first kingdom: He washed their filthy feet by taking the role of a servant.

But they still didn't get it.

Following Jesus and His approach to life frees us from the need to be first. It frees us from the need to feel important. It frees us from needing to get our own way all the time, because following Jesus enables us to put others ahead of ourselves. Of course, that kind of transformation doesn't happen overnight; it takes God's grace to be fully freed from ourselves; it requires practice being Jesus's apprentice in service.

Today's spiritual exercise has two steps. First, read the account of Jesus washing the disciples' feet in John 13:1–20. Second, answer this question: Who do you know that needs their feet washed? OK, not literally. Remember that, by serving, Jesus met a need the disciples had. "Washing someone's feet" might mean doing the dishes tonight instead of waiting for someone to ask you to do it. Maybe it's as simple as sitting next to the lonely kid at school and asking his or her name. Maybe it's helping the older woman across the street by mowing her lawn.

Over time, serving others will remove your need for self-worth, self-help, and self-medication because you will have moved the focus from your**self** to someone else.

Well, duh.

Pray

Jesus, help me live like You did. I want to stop caring so much about what I want. I want to do what You want. Help me put others first. Please show me just one thing I can do to help someone else. Oh, and I'll also need the strength to actually do it; I know that can only come from You.

Reflect

1. Why is it so hard to put someone else's needs first?

2. What is one of your self-centered desires, and how will serving someone else help you combat that selfishness?

3. How will you wash someone's feet? What is the one thing you will do to start practicing the spiritual exercise of service?

GUIDED GROUP DISCUSSION

In Jesus's day, Scripture was kept in synagogues, not in homes. Not on shelves or in desk drawers. Not on phones kept in pockets. And while it's hard for us to imagine having such limited access to the Bible, there are actually still places in the world today where people don't. Places where the Bible is illegal and you'd be arrested for having one in your possession. Places where people are too poor to buy one. Places where the Bible hasn't yet been fully translated—or even partially translated—into the native language.

1. How has easy access to the Bible impacted the way you value it?

2. What should our attitudes be toward reading and memorizing Scripture? What might happen if we surrendered more of our time and attention to it each day?

3. We spend so much time thinking about ourselves, but worship shifts our focus from us to God. It moves us to confess, "You are God and I am not." It also draws us closer to the One who cares for us most.

How does worship help us remember who God is?

How does that make our own lives better?

21

Solitude

We live in such a **noisy** culture. Even when you switch your phone to "silent," it still buzzes every time you get a notification. We also live in an **on-demand** culture. Every piece of entertainment you could want is right at your fingertips. Think about it … when was the last time you even went to the bathroom without your phone? (OK, so maybe you don't have a phone yet. But you get the idea.)

We resist being quiet.

Maybe that's because we're afraid of loneliness.

So, we self-medicate by embracing the noise. Some of us fill our lives with people. Or with entertainment. Or with endless swiping left or right or up or down.

But what if the path away from loneliness is actually … being alone?

Yeah, on the surface that doesn't make sense. Yet it's exactly what Jesus did. In fact, whenever He was facing an important task, Jesus would retreat from the world to spend time with His Father. In **The Chosen**, John the Baptizer said, "You're always running away after performing miracles. Tell me, why do You always go off to these desolate places?"

Season 2,
Episode 5

Jesus's answer is so, so important for us to grasp: "I need solitude."

"And rising very early in the morning, while
it was still dark, he departed and went out
to a desolate place, and there he prayed."
Mark 1:35

"After saying goodbye to them, He
left for the mountain to pray."
Mark 6:46 (NASB)

"But now even more the report
about him went abroad,
and great crowds gathered to hear him
and to be healed of their infirmities.
But he would withdraw to
desolate places and pray."
Luke 5:15–16

"In these days he went out to the mountain to pray,
and all night he continued in prayer to God."
Luke 6:12

"And after he had dismissed the crowds, he
went up on the mountain by himself to pray.
When evening came, he was there alone …"
Matthew 14:23

Jesus demonstrated again and again how to live a life that's intimately connected to God. Choosing to be quiet wasn't a onetime thing. He wasn't just pursuing a little "me time" when He got stressed. The spiritual exercise of solitude—of being **alone** with God with nothing else to distract us—connects us to our Maker, combats our selfishness, and actually comforts us in our loneliness.

And the truth is, we can't just "show up" in life's important moments and expect to perform. The Savior's life and words make clear the correlation:

Jesus practiced solitude to prepare for life.

Finding moments to be alone with God will enable you to follow Him when it matters most. Of course, it's challenging to find opportunities to be alone. But it doesn't have to be a long time— there are countless moments throughout the day when you could get quiet with the Lord. It may mean waking up ten minutes earlier than everyone else. Or opening your Bible instead of turning on the TV before bed. Or you can simply turn off your phone for a bit, perhaps even give it to someone else to hold if that would help you focus on what really matters.

As Jesus demonstrated, the key is to be intentional. And it will be worth it because He's calling you from a noisy life of loneliness into life with Him. You just have to follow His example.

Pray

Father, it's hard to be quiet. Help me listen to You right here, right now.

Reflect

1. Why do you think Jesus spent so much time in solitude?

2. Why don't you spend more time in solitude?

3. How can you be intentional about getting quiet with God today?

Spending Time in Prayer (Part 2)

22

Season 2,
Episode 7

Near the end of season 2, Jesus told His disciples that "prayer is the first step in getting your mind and heart right." They knew prayer was a priority for Him—they saw Him go off on His own to do it plenty of times. So, when they expressed curiosity about what He actually said in those moments, Jesus responded with "Now … now you're behaving like true students."

It was a small but touching moment from the show. And Jesus wants to teach all His apprentices **how** to pray, not just **what** to pray. That's why He gave us the Lord's Prayer—it's a DIY prayer guide. Hopefully you were able to pray it every day for a week, and it's not a bad idea to keep doing it. It can be a helpful way to jump-start your prayer time, a way to remember why we pray in the first place.

So, **how** do we pray? And why did Jesus give us this specific prayer as an example? Let's break it down, line by line:

Our Father in heaven, hallowed be Your name.

Jesus opened His prayer with a little reminder that God is both personal ("our Father") and big enough to handle whatever you bring Him ("in heaven"). **Hallowed** isn't a word we use a lot today, but it means "greatly revered and honored." As Jesus instructed in the episode, you want to start your prayer time by acknowledging God and His greatness.

Your kingdom come, Your will be done, on earth as it is in heaven.

There's so much to learn from this one line. In a way, it sums up Jesus's entire life, ministry, death, and resurrection. His kingdom isn't a faraway place, reserved for you when you die. Instead, when you ask for God's will to be done in your life, you're accessing His kingdom right here, right now, "on earth as it is in heaven."

Give us this day our daily bread.

Hmm. Wonder if there's a gluten-free option? (Sorry, we can't resist a little dad joke every now and then.) To be clear, Jesus wasn't only talking about bread. These words include all our daily needs.

That said, we often treat God like a vending machine. We order up the things we want and hope they fall into our hands when we say amen.

Of course, there's nothing wrong with asking God for things; He wants to hear what's on our minds and in our hearts. And being honest in prayer can actually help us discern the difference between wants and needs since spending time with God (1) connects us to Him and (2) combats our self-centeredness. Which means we can tell Him what we want, and we can ask for what we need, but then we need to trust Him to sort it all out and take care of us.

And forgive us our debts, as we also have forgiven our debtors.

Some Bible versions translate "debts" as "sins" or "trespasses." It's really a combination of all three. When you sin, you're crossing a line you shouldn't—you're trespassing in dangerous territory. So, you ask God to forgive you. But it doesn't stop there, and the next part gets pretty personal.

Has someone trespassed into territory that harmed you? It's important to show them the same grace and forgiveness that God has shown you. So, while you might not forget how you've been wronged, it's important to not let that hurt take over your heart.

And lead us not into temptation, but deliver us from evil.

God wants you to ask for His help to both overcome and avoid situations that tempt you to sin. Temptation will usually strike when you least expect it, and often when your defenses are down. It's important to stay prepared so you can make good choices.

Remember, prayer doesn't always have to sound like a script, and the words you say can be your own. As your circumstances change, so will your prayers. Some days you'll feel sad; other days you'll feel happy—and God welcomes all of it. But Jesus demonstrated that prayer shouldn't be about us alone, as though we're standing in front of a vending machine. Indeed, the Father deserves words of praise, surrender, and trust.

And Jesus showed us how.

Pray

God, You are truly amazing. You love me as Your child, yet You're bigger than I can comprehend. Help me live in Your kingdom and do Your will. I know You'll provide, so please help me to want what You want. Forgive me for stepping off Your path. Father, this next part is hard, so I need Your help. People have hurt me, and I need Your strength to forgive them. Please keep me off that hamster wheel of selfishness so I won't sin.

Reflect

1. What kind of things do you find yourself praying about the most? How are the words both similar and different from the ones Jesus used?

2. Why do you think it's important to start by acknowledging God's greatness?

3. What line from the Lord's Prayer is impacting you the most right now, and why?

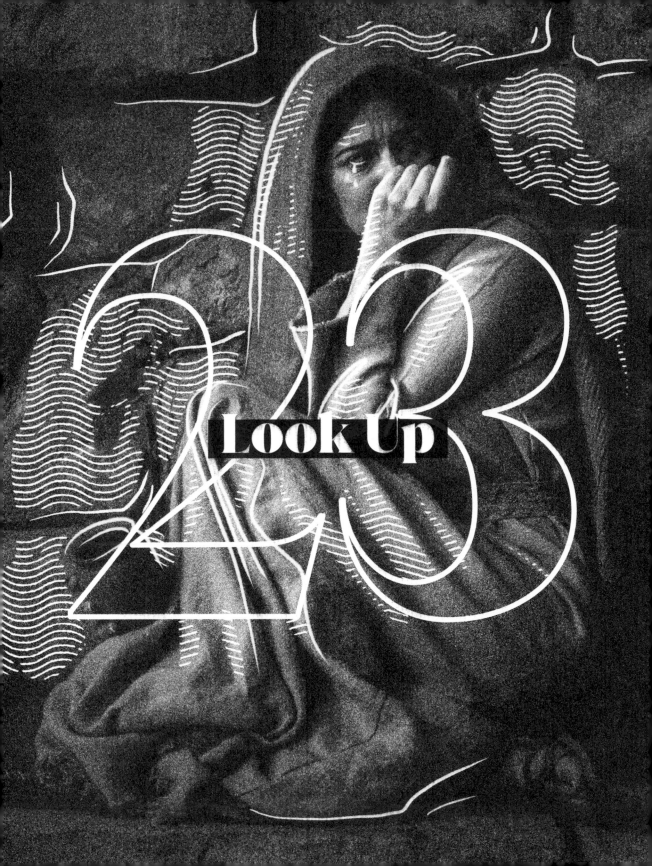

hen you make the choice to follow Jesus, it's often accompanied by emotion—and lots of it. It feels **good** to know our sins are forgiven. There's relief that comes from belonging to God and from knowing we're no longer alone. Most of us are excited to begin our apprenticeship, ready and willing to do whatever it takes to be more like Jesus.

Inevitably, though, excitement fades. Sooner or later, life throws curveballs and we wonder where our good feelings went. We may even question what we believed at the start of our walk with Jesus. If we're not careful, He becomes more like a guy in our rearview mirror, instead of the One who never leaves us or forsakes us (Deuteronomy 31:8).

Truth is, any number of things can throw us off the path, but they all tend to fall into one of two categories. Incidentally, both reveal—once again—the importance of living as Jesus's apprentice.

(1) Painful events. When bad things happen that are outside of our control, our tendency is to focus on rising waters. And those high waters (e.g., stress, worry, fear, confusion, hurt) can cause us to doubt God and even pull away from Him.

(2) Self-focus. We often **choose** to get back on that hamster wheel; we return to our old way of life and all the self-centeredness that comes

> "When you pass through the waters, I will be with you; and through the rivers, they shall not overwhelm you … For I am the Lord your God, the Holy One of Israel, your Savior."
> Isaiah 43:2–3

with it. Of course, as we've been discussing, self-focus and the things we do to self-medicate are really just the "sin which clings so closely." And none of it satisfies our soul.

> "Let us also lay aside every weight, and sin which clings so closely, and let us run with endurance the race that is set before us."
> Hebrews 12:1

Mary Magdalene, no doubt, struggled with old ways too. In season 2, she was triggered by a few things, including the appearance of a demon-possessed man who called her by her old name, Lilith. Shaken, she did what so many of us do: she reverted to the sin that clings so closely. When she finally did return to Jesus, she said, "I just can't live up to it."

"Well, that's true," He replied. "But you don't have to. I just want your heart; the Father just wants your heart. Give us that, which you already have, and the rest will come in time. Did you really think you would never struggle or sin again?"

"I'm just so sorry."

"Look up."

"I can't."

"You can. Look at Me. I forgive you. It's over."

Season 2, Episode 6

The same can be true for you. Jesus just wants your heart. That's it. He invites you to be His apprentice, not to enforce a strict regimen of rules and regulations, but to live in the freedom that comes from following Him.

It's not about being perfect—none of us can be. It's about following. And sometimes as we follow, we're going to trip. Or even fall flat on our faces. But be encouraged, because "if we confess our sins, [Jesus] is faithful and just to forgive us our sins and to cleanse us from all unrighteousness" (1 John 1:9).

When you experience doubt or fear, when you struggle with self-focus or even fall into sinful behavior, when you question where God is in the midst of hard things, there's only one thing to do.

Look up.

"[Let us look] to Jesus, the founder and perfecter
of our faith, who for the joy that was set before
him endured the cross, despising the shame,
and is seated at the right hand of the throne
of God. Consider him who endured from
sinners such hostility against himself, so that
you may not grow weary or fainthearted."
Hebrews 12:2–3

Pray

Jesus, sometimes it's hard to follow You. Some days can be really discouraging, especially when I choose to sin. I know some of my habits are destructive—please help me follow You into the life of freedom You want for me. And when I feel ashamed and broken and unworthy of Your love, please remind me to look up.

Reflect

1. Why do you think Mary returned to her old life?

2. What are some of the bad habits you sometimes return to?

3. Why do you think it's important to look up at Jesus when you feel discouraged or ashamed?

Spending Time in God's Word (Part 2)

You've been taking some pretty big steps down the path of following Jesus. In our first devotional about reading God's Word (page 100), we asked you to do one thing:

Ask God to reveal Himself to you in His Word.

And that's important because opening the Bible isn't like opening a normal book. It's more like opening the doors of a library. Flip to a random page, and there's no telling what you'll find—short stories, long stories, wild stories, gross stories, worship songs, lists of names and law codes, historical records, parables and riddles, dramatic monologues, catchy one-sentence proverbs, even poetry that would make Grandma blush.

Proverb:
a short saying stating
a general truth or
piece of advice.

Because of that, opening the Bible can also be daunting. Luckily, there's no one-size-fits-all approach to encountering God in His Word. In fact, there's all sorts of ways you can tackle it … the key is to **start**. Here's a list of some things you can try:

- Read the "verse of the day" in the YouVersion Bible app every day.
- Read a chapter a day from Luke, then go right into Acts (Luke also wrote Acts, so it's basically a sequel).
- Memorize Bible verses (that's how Jesus "exercised" to prepare for temptation in Matthew 4).

- Start a reading plan (again, YouVersion has a lot of these!).
- Get a reading buddy and text each other each time you start reading.
- Pick a topic and study what the Bible has to say about it (you can even Google "Bible verses about _____ ").

For today, we've got something else we want you to try that's designed to help you fight the noise and distractions that usually interrupt your time in God's Word. Simply follow the steps as you read through the passage below:

Step 1: Listen

Read the entire passage aloud … **slowly**. Listen for any word or phrase that stands out to you. Sometimes it helps to write it down.

Step 2: Reflect

Now read the passage aloud again. Think about that special word or phrase from step 1. Ponder it, think about it, turn it over in your mind. You don't have to analyze it; instead, we're trying to reflect on what God is saying to us in His Word. And sometimes it takes a minute for stuff to sink in.

Step 3: Respond

Now read the entire passage aloud a third time. Ask God how He wants you to respond to this word or phrase. Again, it might be helpful to write down what you're thinking or working through.

Step 4: Contemplate

Stick with us, you're almost there! Now read the entire passage aloud a final time … and **shhh** … just listen. You want to quiet your heart and mind. Don't say anything, don't pray anything, just rest in God's Word.

OK, here we go …

"In the beginning was the Word, and the Word was with God, and the Word was God. He was in the beginning with God. All things were made through him, and without him was not any thing made that was made. In him was life, and the life was the light of men. The light shines in the darkness, and the darkness has not overcome it."

John 1:1–5

John called Jesus "the Word" to help us understand His role in creation. In the beginning He spoke and everything in the world came to be. His words are powerful. His words are like light that chases away darkness. His words drive out fear and confusion. His words bring comfort and understanding. His words reveal what's true and what's actually important. Jesus is the Word.

Pray

You've already done it.

Reflect

Again, you've already done it.

Week 6

GUIDED GROUP DISCUSSION

1. Focusing on others is the easiest way to not focus on ourselves. And that should be our goal because Jesus said, "Whoever would be great among you must be your servant, and whoever would be first among you must be your slave, even as the Son of Man came not to be served but to serve, and to give his life as a ransom for many" (Matthew 20:26–28).

Why are we so resistant to service? How does helping others actually benefit **us**?

2. Why do you suppose we humans try so hard to avoid solitude? Why did Jesus pursue it?

3. Jesus wants your heart. He invites you to be His apprentice, not to enforce rules and regulations, but to live in the freedom that comes from giving Him your heart.

How do spiritual exercises like praying, worshipping, reading your Bible, and spending time with God help you surrender your heart consistently and fully to Him? How does practicing these exercises actually help us to experience freedom?

Part 3

Bringing Your Burdens to Jesus

Come to Me
All You
Who Are Weary

All you who are weary ..." That's a lot of us. For a lot of different reasons. But while circumstances may vary from person to person, all hard things eventually lead to the same place:

Weariness.

To be weary means to be exhausted in strength, endurance, enthusiasm—or faith. Yeah, we said it. Hard things can weaken our faith and cause us to question who the Bible says God is.

God is love (1 John 4:16). God is kind (Titus 3:4–6). God is ever-present (Psalm 139:7–12). God is faithful (2 Timothy 2:13). God is merciful (Psalm 145:8–9). God is powerful (Jeremiah 32:17). God is wise (Psalm 147:5).

God is ... God is ... God is ...

Except, what about all the times it feels like He isn't?

Stick a pin in that.

Truth is, a lot of people say a lot of things about God—some positive, some really, really negative. And we suppose that can be partially explained by circumstances. Meaning, if you've had positive experiences in your life, you're more likely to like God. If you've had negative experiences in your life, you're more likely to **not** like God and to dismiss Him as either non-caring or not-able or non-existent.

> "Stick a pin in that" is an old-person saying that means "hold that thought" or "we'll get back to that."

Then again, there are those crazy people who've had really bad experiences but still manage to find ongoing comfort, peace, wholeness, and fullness in Jesus. To find rest for their weary souls.

How? Where does faith like that come from?

Well, ironically, from experience.

Life is hard in a thousand ways because sin has wrecked the world in a thousand ways. Everything from the environment to the family unit; from how we interact with one another to what we do when no one is watching; from our physical bodies to the deepest parts of our hearts … we've made a mess of things. And nothing will be truly fixed until Jesus comes back and restores creation to the way it was supposed to be.

But in the meantime, Jesus offers us rest. Which means He hasn't left us to struggle on our own. Instead, He says, "Come to me, all you who are weary and burdened, and I will give you rest. Take my yoke upon you and learn from me, for I am gentle and humble in heart, and you will find

Season 3,
Episode 8

Want to know what it'll be like when Jesus comes back and restores creation? Isaiah 65:17–25 (NLT) gives us a good idea:

"Look! I am creating new
heavens and a new earth,
and no one will even think about
the old ones anymore.
Be glad; rejoice forever in my creation! …
No longer will babies die when
only a few days old. No longer will
adults die before they have lived a
full life. No longer will people be
considered old at one hundred! …
In those days people will live in the
houses they build and eat the fruit of their
own vineyards. Unlike the past, invaders
will not take their houses and confiscate
their vineyards. For my people will live
as long as trees, and my chosen ones will
have time to enjoy their hard-won gains.
They will not work in vain,
and their children will not be
doomed to misfortune.
For they are people blessed by the LORD,
and their children, too, will be blessed.
I will answer them before they
even call to me. While they are still
talking about their needs, I will go
ahead and answer their prayers!
The wolf and the lamb will feed together.
The lion will eat hay like a cow.…
In those days no one will be hurt or
destroyed on my holy mountain.
I, the LORD, have spoken!"

rest for your souls. For my yoke is easy and my burden is light" (Matthew 11:28–30 NIV).

That kind of exchange—our weariness for Jesus's strength; our heavy, heart-rending burdens for His comfort—only happens when we muster what measly faith we **do** have and enter into His presence. When we sit with Him, our hearts and hands open. When we confess our inability to carry our burdens alone. When we profess that He's the only One who can really help.

In those quiet moments, something happens, not necessarily to our circumstances, but to our ability to endure them: Jesus takes our burdens and gives us His yoke instead.

So, what's a yoke? Well, in Bible times a wooden yoke joined two animals together, allowing them to combine strength in order to pull a heavy load. By itself, an ox or horse had no rest from grueling work, no help in exhaustion, no options when it all became too much—they just had to plow ahead.

Jesus is offering to be yoked to you. He's offering to help carry your load. To bring His otherworldly strength, love, kindness, faithfulness, mercy, power, and wisdom to your circumstances.

By yourself, you'll have no help. No rest from the grueling world, no help in exhaustion, no option when your circumstances become too much.

But with Him, you'll have Him. Experiencing His presence in the midst of your circumstances will increase your faith and allow you to not only endure, but to also believe God is all the things the Bible says He is.

"Have you not known? Have you not heard? The
LORD is the everlasting God, the Creator of the
ends of the earth. He does not faint or grow
weary; his understanding is unsearchable.
He gives power to the faint, and to him who
has no might he increases strength.

Even youths shall faint and be weary, and young
men shall fall exhausted; but they who wait for
the LORD shall renew their strength; they shall
mount up with wings like eagles; they shall run
and not be weary; they shall walk and not faint."
Isaiah 40:28–31

Pray

Lord, life can really be too much for me sometimes. I admit I'm struggling to carry my burdens alone. Honestly, I wish You would just take them away—I wish that You'd use Your power to fix what's broken. Help me trust Your wisdom and timing while I wait for that day. Help me to believe You're all the things the Bible says You are. And help me accept the offer to be yoked to You, Jesus. With Your supernatural strength, please help carry this load.

Reflect

1. What burdens are you carrying?

2. How have your experiences shaped the way you view God?

3. Are you willing to come into His presence and experience something new?

26

Fasting

Yeah, we're tempted to skip this subject too. So, let's just put it out there:

Fasting isn't fun.

It's not normal, either. Meaning, it's not a thing our bodies are naturally programmed to do. Going without food doesn't make much sense because, not only do we like eating, we need food to live. Although, that's actually the point.

Fasting is an exercise to help us become more dependent on God for everyday living.

It's another way to bring our burdens to Him.

Don't worry. We're not going to suggest you stop eating for forty days like Jesus did (Matthew 4:1–11). Instead, we're just going to look at what Jesus said about fasting and consider how it might apply to us.

During the Sermon on the Mount, Jesus criticized how some of the people were fasting. "And when you fast, do not look gloomy like the hypocrites, for they disfigure their faces that their fasting may be seen by others" (Matthew 6:16).

Notice He didn't say **if** you fast, He said **when**—which doesn't really make fasting seem optional. Also, Jesus clearly wanted people to fast for the right reasons and not to impress each other, as though fasting makes the fast**er** more "spiritual" than everyone else. "But when you fast, anoint your head and wash your face, that your fasting may **not** be seen by others but by your Father who is in secret. And your Father who sees in secret will reward you" (verses 17–18).

Ugh. There's that word again … **when**.

But there's another word there too … **reward**.

Jesus clearly stated that the Father will reward you for fasting. Which means the exercise of fasting isn't really about skipping a meal, but about getting a reward. Of course, we fast to remind our bodies who we're truly dependent on. We fast to establish God at the center of our lives. We fast to find freedom from self-medication. We fast to follow in the footsteps of Jesus.

But we also fast to get a reward.

More on that in a minute.

What do you need to fast from? What if, for one day, you fasted from TV and dedicated that time to God? Or what if you fasted from social media for a weekend (gasp)?

Truth is, technology has changed you. That's not speculation, it's a scientific fact. There are countless studies on how using social media actually triggers dopamine, the chemical your body creates to reward behavior. There's also a thing called PVS—that's when your brain tricks you into thinking your phone is vibrating when it's actually not (yikes!). And so, intentionally unplugging from tech for a period of time might be exactly what your heart and mind need.

> PVS = phantom vibration syndrome

But we digress.

Regardless of what you choose to fast from, your urges can act as reminders to move toward Jesus. To pray. To praise. To read your Bible. To reach out to someone who might need a kind word. To rest. To lean into the Lord, declaring your dependency on Him and freedom from everything else.

By entrusting yourself to the Lord, even when it comes to something as important as food, you're ensuring a reward: **that the God who sees what you do in secret will draw near.**

And there's literally nothing more soul satisfying than that.

> "Draw near to God, and he will draw near to you. Cleanse your hands, you sinners, and purify your hearts, you double-minded.... Humble yourselves before the Lord, and he will exalt you."
> James 4:8, 10

In context we see that Jesus was teaching about fasting from food, not Instagram. We encourage you to explore fasting from food for a short time and as long as you don't already struggle with an eating disorder. Make sure you talk to an adult about fasting the **right** way. Each person's body responds differently, so it's important to think it through and have a plan.

Pray

Father, You are so good. You hold the weight of the world in Your hands, yet You care deeply for me. You alone know what I need. I've become dependent on so many things that **aren't** You. Help me know what I need to fast from, Father. Then give me the strength to do it, because I know I can't do it on my own.

Reflect

1. Why do you think Jesus fasted from food for forty days and nights before starting His public ministry?

2. Why is it so hard to fast? How does the idea of fasting make you feel?

3. What do you need to fast from? Write it down. How long should you fast from it? Remember, it's OK to start small.

27

Becoming One

On the night before He died, Jesus prayed an incredible prayer for His followers. Similar to the Lord's Prayer, He began by acknowledging the greatness of God—and then He continued for a full eleven verses before making this prayer request: "Holy Father, keep them in your name, which you have given me, **that they may be one, even as we are one"** (John 17:11).

Wow. It's hard to comprehend what it would be like to experience "oneness" with others in the same way Jesus and the Father are one. Yet, the fact is, you were created for that kind of community. You were created with a desire to be fully accepted without judgment, to be truly known, to be unconditionally loved. A desire to not only share life with others, but to have a shared purpose as well.

That's what Jesus wants for His followers. A little bit further into His prayer, He made this request on **your** behalf: "I do not ask for these only, but also for those who will believe in me through their word, that they may all be one, just as you, Father, are in me, and I in you, that they also may be in us, so that the world may believe that you have sent me" (verses 20–21).

You can feel it, right? That hunger for meaningful connection, a yearning for something more, an instinctive ache to experience the oneness Jesus prayed for.

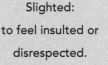

Season 1,
Episode 7

Season 2,
Episodes 1, 7

Yet we struggle to attain it, just like the early disciples did.

The men who followed Jesus consistently bickered about which one of them would be greater in heaven (Luke 22:24–26) and often misunderstood the nature of Jesus's kingdom. Throughout the show we saw that play out. Simon protested when Jesus called Matthew. The "Sons of Thunder" wanted to call down fire from the heavens when they felt slighted. And Andrew harshly judged Mary Magdalene for slipping back into her old habits. (Just to name a few.)

> Slighted:
> to feel insulted or
> disrespected.

If the people who actually saw Jesus face to face struggled to achieve oneness, how are **we** ever gonna do it? Look around your church (or **any** church, for that matter) … it's easy to find examples of people not getting along.

Perhaps it would help us to think of oneness as a direction we're headed in together instead of a destination we have to arrive at. The journey to being one is long and takes effort. But just like our other spiritual exercises, there are things you can do to experience oneness along the way.

First, you need to be intentional about sharing life with other apprentices. This might be in a Bible study or small group, but being part of a community is a nonnegotiable part of following Jesus. See if there's a prayer group that meets at your school. If you're unable to gather in person, join an online Christian community that meets regularly in order to go deeper together in Jesus.

Bottom line: you just can't follow Him by yourself because you'll need support, encouragement, accountability, and guidance from others. Indeed, God gives us people to help carry our burdens. So, if you don't have a community yet, take a look around. Chances are you'll find someone who needs it as much as you do, and that's a great place to start.

Second, the spiritual exercises you're learning to do alone should also be practiced as a group. Bible reading and prayer should be on the agenda, but there are other things you can do together, like worship, confession, forgiveness, and good ole-fashioned serving. Because whether it's a missions trip or helping old folks with their yard work, when followers of Jesus serve together, it creates a unique form of oneness … because we're accomplishing the last part of Jesus's prayer:

"So that the world may believe that you have sent me" (John 17:21).

> "Let us hold fast the confession of our hope without wavering, for he who promised is faithful. And let us consider how to stir up one another to love and good works, not neglecting to meet together, as is the habit of some, but encouraging one another, and all the more as you see the Day drawing near."
> Hebrews 10:23–25

> "For where two or three are gathered in my name, there am I among them."
> Matthew 18:20

Pray

Father, You are an incredible Creator. You made the heavens and the earth and everything in them. And You made me. You planted within my heart the desire to know others the way You know me, to be one with them as You are one. But it isn't easy. I even have a hard time with some of the kids in my church. Help me see them the way You do … the way You see me, Father. Help me create the kind of community Jesus prayed for.

Reflect

1. Why do you think the disciples had such a hard time understanding the unity Jesus wanted for His followers? Why do you think people in churches today still struggle?

2. What are some of the biggest obstacles to being one?

3. What are some of the spiritual exercises you'd like to see your community practice more often? What can you do to help your community?

28

Not What
You Were

The saying "Burn the ships" dates back to 1519, when the captain of a Spanish expedition to Mexico ordered his crew to burn their **own** ships upon arrival. He knew his men were exhausted from the long journey and that they might be tempted to turn back—which meant they needed motivation to dig deep and soldier on. So, he created a situation where quitting wasn't an option; the men would have to conquer their enemies in the New World or die.

You know … because they burned the ships.

Fast-forward to you, right here, right now, reading this devotional. Chances are you don't think you have much in common with centuries-old Spanish invaders, but you actually do, because when you follow Jesus, turning back is no longer an option. You'll have to dig deep and soldier on. You'll have to burn the ships.

Season 3,
Episode 2

"If we've left the country where sin is sovereign, how can we still live in our old house there? Or didn't you realize we packed up and left there for good? That is what happened in baptism. When we went under the water, we left the old country of sin behind; when we came up out of the water, we entered into the new country of grace—a new life in a new land!"

Romans 6:2–3 (MSG)

There will be times when you're tempted to look back, either because you miss your old way of life or because you're still haunted by the shame it holds. Both have the power to distract you and get your focus off Jesus. But two things are true: (1) the freedom you desire is only found in Him, and (2) once you belong to Him, you're no longer what you were.

In **The Chosen**, we watched Jesus pair up the disciples in order to send them out. We listened as He instructed them to preach and heal and prepare the hearts of people—and to burn their ships. Because not only were they going to have to 100 percent rely on God's provision and protection—which was a totally new way of living—they were also going to have to "forget what lies behind and strain toward what's ahead."

Their conversation went like this:

JESUS: Matthew and Z …
(All of the men seem surprised. Concerned. Confused … except for—)
Z: What?
SIMON: Rabbi, You sure about this?
JESUS (continuing as though everyone in the room isn't gobsmacked …): Go all the way down to Jericho. I know it's near Samaria, but you'll be fine.

"But thanks be to God, that you who were once slaves of sin have become obedient from the heart to the standard of teaching to which you were committed, and, having been set free from sin, have become slaves of righteousness."
Romans 6:17–18

"Forgetting what lies behind and straining forward to what lies ahead, I press on toward the goal for the prize of the upward call of God in Christ Jesus."
Philippians 3:13–14

Gobsmacked: utterly astonished, astounded.

(Z is still confused. Matthew is still nervous. Everyone else is still wide-eyed.)

JESUS: Z, everyone is reacting to the notion of you traveling with a tax collector.

Z: What?

JESUS: We have not told you about Matthew's former occupation.

Z: He's a tax collector??

JESUS: He's no more a tax collector than you are a Zealot. Listen to Me … none of you is what you were. Remember that, all of you. And, Z, you and Matthew will be able to remember that better than anyone else.

None of you is what you were.
None of you is what you were.
None of you is what you were.

Let that sink in for a minute. Because, just like the disciples, once you choose to follow Jesus, you're a new person because you're remade in the image of the One you're following. Which means your identity, your purpose, and your hope lie **ahead** of you, not behind.

Pray

Jesus, thank You for new beginnings. Thank You for offering freedom from sin and shame. Please help me to stop looking back and to fix my eyes on You

---

If you haven't yet chosen to follow Jesus, now is as good a time as any! Pray this prayer to help you get started: Jesus, I believe You're the Son of God who came to earth as a sacrifice for my sins. I'm sorry for my sin, Lord. Please forgive me and save me and keep me. I want to follow You. Please show me how … I surrender. Amen.

and the path ahead of us. It's hard sometimes … so I'm going to need Your help each day, each step. Thank You for Your promise to stay with me and to remake me in Your image.

Reflect

1. What do you tend to look back at?

2. In what ways does shame keep you stuck and even vulnerable to sinning again?

Read the verses in the margin that deal directly with shame …

What does the Bible say God does once you ask for His forgiveness?

"For I will be merciful toward their iniquities, and I will remember their sins no more."
Hebrews 8:12

Iniquities:
wicked or immoral acts.

"[God] does not deal with us according to our sins, nor repay us according to our iniquities. For as high as the heavens are above the earth, so great is his steadfast love toward those who fear him; as far as the east is from the west, so far does he remove our transgressions from us."
Psalm 103:10–12

Transgressions:
wicked or immoral acts.

3. Why does Jesus want us to keep our eyes on Him alone?

"Now if we have died with Christ, we believe that we
will also live with him. We know that Christ, being
raised from the dead, will never die again; death no
longer has dominion over him. For the death he died
he died to sin, once for all, but the life he lives he
lives to God. So you also must consider yourselves
dead to sin and alive to God in Christ Jesus."
Romans 6:8–11

Week 7

GUIDED GROUP DISCUSSION

1. Jesus says, "Come to me, all you who are weary and burdened, and I will give you rest. Take my yoke upon you and learn from me, for I am gentle and humble in heart, and you will find rest for your souls. For my yoke is easy and my burden is light" (Matthew 11:28–30 NIV).

When we become yoked to Jesus, when we exchange our weariness for Jesus's strength, our heavy, heart-rending burdens for His comfort, what happens to our circumstances **even if they don't change**?

2. How do exercises like fasting and becoming connected to other believers actually help **relieve** our burdens?

3. Take a moment to listen to the old hymn "I Have Decided to Follow Jesus" (we like the version by Elevation Worship). Or the newer song from For King & Country, "Burn the Ships."

That's all. Just listen. And worship. And resolve to burn the ships.

As we've mentioned, the first disciples were a very strange and interesting collection of people. Together, they could never have been called "Jesus's School for the Gifted." No, a far better title would've been "Jesus's School of Misfit Apprentices"—because they totally were. But since we're still talking about them over two thousand years later, it's safe to say Jesus knew what He was doing. And despite their level of misfit-ness, Jesus sent them out.

"[Jesus] called to him his twelve disciples and gave them authority over unclean spirits, to cast them out, and to heal every disease and every affliction" (Matthew 10:1).

Um … what the what? Jesus wanted **these** guys to do the same kinds of things He was doing? At that moment, the boys were still expecting the Messiah to fight Rome. They were still arguing about who among them was the greatest. They were still not fully understanding Jesus's teachings. Still not quite getting … well … a lot.

No doubt, they—like us—were surprised to be sent.

BIG JAMES: You're sending **us**?
ANDREW: I don't understand.
MATTHEW: Could You just repeat that one more time?
PHILIP: Heal the sick?
THADDAEUS: Cast out demons?

Season 3,
Episode 2

NATHANAEL: Was there a ceremony I missed?
JOHN: … we're not nearly qualified …

Can you blame them? You'd be freaking out too if suddenly you went from apprentice to apostle—if graduation day was unexpectedly thrust upon you. Nevertheless, Jesus was sending His followers out to tell people about Him, to teach and heal and witness in His name.

But the invitation to be a disciple is open to everyone; characters of all shapes and sizes are welcome. But how will they know unless those of us who follow Jesus **tell them**? Which is why graduation day comes for us all. In fact, the moment we sign up to be Jesus's apprentices, we become His messengers. We might not fully understand all of His teachings yet, but that's been true of every new disciple since the first twelve were called!

And like them, we have a mission:

Tell people about Jesus.

While being His messenger might feel intimidating at first, the story itself is easy because it's **yours**. Think about it: you were one way, and now you're completely different. And you get to tell people what happened in between. That's really all there is to it. You might not think you're ready, and that's OK. We all feel that way sometimes.

Just remember what Jesus told Nathanael:

"I don't need you to feel anything to do great things."

Apostle literally means "one who's sent."

"Do not be anxious how you are to speak or what you are to say, for what you are to say will be given to you in that hour. For it is not you who speak, but the Spirit of your Father speaking through you."
Matthew 10:19–20

Pray

Jesus, I'm just getting used to the idea of following and living like You—but becoming Your messenger takes this thing to a whole new level. I want to tell my friends about You, I do. I'm just not sure how. I don't feel confident yet. And truthfully, I'm a little scared of what others will think. Help me overcome my fear so that I can invite others to follow You too.

Reflect

1. It's hard to believe Jesus built His church with such a collection of misfits. Why do you think He chose them to be His messengers?

2. Why do you think it's so hard to tell others about Jesus?

3. Who are some of the people in your life that would benefit from following Jesus?

30

You Will Be Healed

You might feel a little different than everyone around you. Maybe they dress or act differently than you do.

Or you might feel **a lot** different than everyone around you. Maybe they walk or talk differently. Maybe they look, hear, or see differently. Or maybe they think or communicate differently than you do.

Maybe you're not able to be or do any of the things others consider "normal." And even though America's Declaration of Independence says that **all men are created equal**, you don't have to look very far to see it's not completely true because some people are born into extreme poverty. Others are born with different brain chemistry. Others are confined to wheelchairs. Still others are disfigured.

The list goes on and on. And on. And none of it sounds very "equal."

In **The Chosen**, Little James walked with a limp. At the time, doctors wouldn't have known about conditions like scoliosis or cerebral palsy—although those would be the proper diagnoses today. Of course, we don't actually know if any of the disciples walked with a limp. And we don't know that they didn't. The purpose of the show's storyline is simply to help us put ourselves in the disciples' shoes, including all the things that make us different.

Season 3,
Episode 2

In a television show, it would be easy to remedy Little James's situation. After all, Jesus healed a lot of people of a lot of things, and

it always made for a great story. And Jesus is still healing today …
though not everyone, which is why so many people
throughout the course of history have asked the same
gut-wrenching question:

Why do some people get healed and others don't?

Well, that's a toughie, and we're not going to
pretend otherwise.

LITTLE JAMES: I wanted to ask You a question.

JESUS: Please.

LITTLE JAMES: You're sending us out with the ability
to heal the sick and lame … that is what You said.

JESUS: Yes.

LITTLE JAMES: So You're telling me that I have
the ability to heal. (*Jesus nods, though He knows
what's coming.*) Forgive me, I just find that difficult
to imagine with my condition … which You haven't
healed.

JESUS (*stepping toward Little James—*): Do you
want to be healed?

LITTLE JAMES (*hopeful—*): Yes—of course! If that's
possible …

JESUS: I think you've seen enough to know it's
possible.

LITTLE JAMES: Then why haven't You?

JESUS: Because I trust you.

LITTLE JAMES: What?

Remember, the show isn't Scripture; it's historical fiction **steeped** in Scripture. So, while the words in the script aren't Bible verses, here are some that back up the way we chose to tell Little James's story.

"Truly, truly, I say to you, whoever believes in me will also do the works that I do; and greater works than these will he do, because I am going to the Father."
John 14:12

"Three times I pleaded with the Lord about [my condition], that it should leave me. But he said to me, 'My grace is sufficient for you, for my power is made perfect in weakness.'"
2 Corinthians 12:8–9

JESUS: Little James. Precious little James ... I need you to listen to me very carefully, because what I'm going to say defines your whole life to this point, and will define the rest of your life. Do you understand? *(James nods, eager.)* In the Father's will I could heal you right now. And you'd have a good story to tell, yes?

LITTLE JAMES: Yes! That You do miracles.

JESUS: And that's a good story. But there are already dozens who can tell that story, and there will be hundreds more, even thousands. But think of the story that you'll have if I don't heal you ... to know how to proclaim that you still praise God in spite of this. To know how to focus on all that matters, so much more than the body.

To show people that you can be patient with your suffering here on earth because you know you'll spend eternity with no suffering. Not everyone can understand that. How many people do you think the Father and I trust with this?

LITTLE JAMES: I know it's easy to say the song of David, "I'm fearfully and wonderfully made," but it doesn't make it easier. And in this group, it doesn't make me feel like any less of a burden.

"For nothing will be impossible with God."
Luke 1:37

"And this is the confidence that we have toward him, that if we ask anything ***according to his will*** he hears us. And if we know that he hears us in whatever we ask, we know that we have the requests that we have asked of him."
1 John 5:14–15

"For I have learned in whatever situation I am to be content. I know how to be brought low, and I know how to abound. In any and every circumstance, I have learned the secret of facing plenty and hunger, abundance and need. I can do all things through him who strengthens me."
Philippians 4:11–13

JESUS: A burden? First of all, it's far easier to deal with your slow walking than it is to deal with Simon's temper, trust Me.

(Little James laughs through his tears.)

JESUS: Are you fast? Do you look impressive when you walk? No, but those are the things the Father doesn't care about. You are going to do more for Me than most people ever dream. So many people need healing in order to believe in Me, or they need healing because their hearts are so sick. That doesn't apply to you.

And many are healed, or not healed, because the Father in heaven has a certain plan for them that may be a mystery …

When you pass from this earth, and you meet your Father in heaven where Isaiah promises you will leap like a deer, your reward will be great. So hold on a little longer. And when you discover yourself finding true strength because of your weakness, and you do great things in My name in spite of this, the impact will last for generations.

Do you understand?

(Little James nods.)

JESUS: And, James, remember … you will be healed.

It's only a matter of time.

"He will wipe away every tear from their eyes, and death shall be no more, neither shall there be mourning, nor crying, nor pain anymore, for the former things have passed away."
Revelation 21:4

"For you formed my inward parts; you knitted me together in my mother's womb. I praise you, for I am fearfully and wonderfully made. Wonderful are your works; my soul knows it very well. My frame was not hidden from you, when I was being made in secret, intricately woven in the depths of the earth. Your eyes saw my unformed substance; in your book were written, every one of them, the days that were formed for me, when as yet there was none of them."
Psalm 139:13–16

Pray

Father, You created the universe and You also created me. I don't really understand why pain exists in the world. I don't know why You heal some people and not others. But I know that one day, no matter what, You will heal everyone, including me. Give me courage to ask for healing now, but also strength to trust and hold on until You wipe the tears from my eyes.

Reflect

1. Why is it significant that Jesus would use someone like Little James? For Him to include people in His work with maladies of all different kinds?

2. What did you think about Little James's conversation with Jesus?

"But the LORD said to Samuel, 'Do not look on his appearance or on the height of his stature, because I have rejected him. For the LORD sees not as man sees: man looks on the outward appearance, but the LORD looks on the heart.'"
1 Samuel 16:7

"For my thoughts are not your thoughts, neither are your ways my ways, declares the LORD. For as the heavens are higher than the earth, so are my ways higher than your ways and my thoughts than your thoughts."
Isaiah 55:8–9

"Therefore I will boast all the more gladly of my weaknesses, so that the power of Christ may rest upon me. For the sake of Christ, then, I am content with weaknesses, insults, hardships, persecutions, and calamities. For when I am weak, then I am strong."
2 Corinthians 12:9–10

3. Explain the following statement: Knowing about your future in heaven should impact the way you feel about your present circumstances on earth.

"They shall hunger no more, neither thirst anymore; the sun shall not strike them, nor any scorching heat. For [Jesus] the Lamb in the midst of the throne will be their shepherd, and he will guide them to springs of living water, and God will wipe away every tear from their eyes."

Revelation 7:16–17

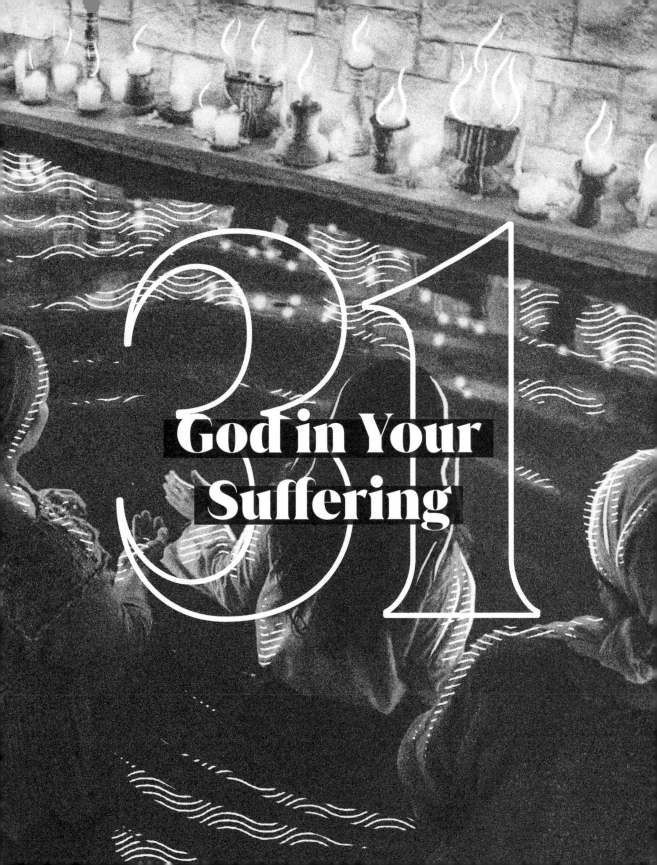

31

God in Your
Suffering

The **Chosen** portrayed a lot of suffering. Little James had to accept his physical disability and still follow Jesus. John the Baptizer sat in prison. Jairus lost his daughter. Gaius's son grew ill. Veronica experienced both physical affliction and social isolation.

And Eden. Oh, Eden. What she endured … there's no quick fix, no magic wand that could make pain like that go away.

Same is true for you.

We're confident you've experienced pain and hurt and loneliness at some point in your life. Maybe not right now. Maybe not even recently. But you've felt the sting of suffering—everyone has to some degree or another. You might not be physically disabled. You might not have been falsely imprisoned. You might not understand the feeling of helplessness—and hopelessness—that Simon endured as he watched Eden suffer such loss. But that doesn't minimize what **you've** been through. It doesn't lessen your own suffering.

Pain is pain is pain. And it begs the question:

Where exactly is God in the pain of it all?

We'll get to that in a minute. But first, it's important to know that suffering isn't a punishment. Yes, sin introduced suffering into God's creation—it's what caused the mess we continually find ourselves in. And your sin can definitely lead to painful consequences. But God doesn't sit up in heaven keeping score, punishing you for every bad thought

Season 3,
Episodes 1, 2, 5, 6

or deed. On the contrary, Psalm 103:10–12 tells us, "He does not deal with us according to our sins, nor repay us according to our iniquities … as far as the east is from the west, so far does he remove our transgressions from us."

If God is compassionate toward us **even in our sin**, where is He in our suffering?

1. God understands your pain.

Jesus put on skin, learned to speak our language, hung out down the street, attended school, and had to work His father's trade. While on earth, He endured physical, emotional, and spiritual anguish. He knows what it is to feel the sting of loss, rejection, and betrayal. To endure pain unimaginable.

2. Jesus stays with you in your suffering.

Experiencing pain doesn't mean that He's abandoned you; it's actually the opposite! The author of **The Chronicles of Narnia** put it this way: "God whispers to us in our pleasures, speaks in our conscience, but shouts in our pain: it is His megaphone to rouse a deaf world." When we suffer, God is there, listening, watching, grieving, and waiting for relief right along with us.

3. Suffering can lead you closer to God …

or further away. The book of Job in the Old Testament tells an incredible story about a man who lost everything. As his world was crumbling

> "Have this mind among yourselves, which is yours in Christ Jesus, who, though he was in the form of God, did not count equality with God a thing to be grasped, but emptied himself, by taking the form of a servant, being born in the likeness of men. And being found in human form, he humbled himself by becoming obedient to the point of death, even death on a cross."
> Philippians 2:5–8

> "The LORD is near to the brokenhearted and saves the crushed in spirit."
> Psalm 34:18

around him, even his wife yelled, "Curse God and die!" In other words, just give up! But Job knew that would be the pathway to bitterness and resentment. Even after so much loss, Job found a way to hold on to his faith … and it led him into a deeper relationship with the God who loved him and did ultimately rescue, redeem, and restore him.

It was only a matter of time. And on that note …

4. **God's timing is perfect.** As the saying goes, **God is seldom early, but He is never late**. Just when Job thought he couldn't endure anything more, God answered his cries. And that's the pattern we see again and again in the Bible: God shows up, in His wisdom and exactly on time.

And He'll show up for you too. It probably won't be exactly when you ask Him to; He understands the things you don't, and He's working all things for your good and for His glory.

Which means His timing will be perfect.

The clouds **will** eventually break.

The sun **will** shine through.

Because God will never abandon you to suffering.

Pray

Father, You formed the heavens and the earth, You created the world and everything in it, so You alone know what I need. You alone can heal my heart. I know You understand my suffering, so help me turn to You and trust You. I have so many

> "Job answered the LORD and said: 'I know that you can do all things, and that no purpose of yours can be thwarted…. I had heard of you by the hearing of the ear, but now my eye sees you.'"
> Job 42:1–5

> "Do not overlook this one fact, beloved, that with the Lord one day is as a thousand years, and a thousand years as one day. The Lord is not slow to fulfill his promise as some count slowness, but is patient toward you, not wishing that any should perish, but that all should reach repentance."
> 2 Peter 3:8–9

questions, God. But instead of looking for immediate answers and relief on demand, help me to seek and find You instead.

Reflect

1. What do you think about the quote from C. S. Lewis? Why is pain "God's megaphone"?

2. Why is it important to turn to God and not away from Him when you are suffering?

3. The book of Job is pretty long, but reading God's response to Job's questions can really put things in perspective. Try reading Job 38–42. What does this tell us about the nature of God? How might knowing these things about God help us when we're hurting?

Side note: Encountering God won't answer all your questions. He might not explain why you've had to suffer; He didn't answer Job's many questions either. But what He **did** give was so much better because Job got to experience God's presence in the midst of suffering. And that's more satisfying than anything else our hearts desire.

Blessings in this life are icing on the cake.
The cake, dear reader, is relationship with God.

32

You (Don't)
Got This

You're in the home stretch now—only five devotionals left. You've made it **so far** in this book … hopefully you've been challenged, inspired, and encouraged. We didn't pull any punches; we didn't pretend that life will be easy now or that faith is a magic wand. But we hope—through the Bible, the show, and this book—you've seen how much better life with Jesus is than what the world has to offer.

Unfortunately, even after you've chosen to follow Jesus, it's easy to get distracted and pulled off course, to start focusing on the waters as they rise around you instead of the God who wants to rescue you from them. So, today, we want to take a step back and allow you to come up for air. We want you to be encouraged.

To that end, we're tempted to say, "You got this!" Buuuuut, that's not actually true.

You don't got this.

That's the whole point of this whole book. It's also the whole point of **The Chosen**, because the truth is that no amount of self-help, self-motivation, or self-medication can do for you what Jesus can do for you.

And there's incredible freedom in knowing that.

Season 3,
Episode 8

Episode 8 of season 3 came to an emotional finish as multiple characters—especially Eden and Simon—shifted their focus from the waters that overwhelm back to Jesus. Psalm 77 puts an exclamation point on their experience, reminding us that **none of us got this**.

But the One we follow does.

"The crash of your thunder was in the whirlwind;
your lightnings lighted up the world; the
earth trembled and shook. Your way was
through the sea, your path through the great
waters; yet your footprints were unseen."
Psalm 77:18–19

There will be a time when your world will tremble. It will be shaken.
But **He** will take you through the sea.
And **He** will take you through the "great waters."
Not you.
You don't got this.
But Jesus does.

Pray

God, You part the waters. You take me through the sea. Thank You for being the One who's got this, because I know I don't. Thank You.

Reflect

Be encouraged. God's got this. He's got **you**.

GUIDED GROUP DISCUSSION

1. Why is it vital to tell others about Jesus? And before you answer, think about all the things we've been talking about and studying in this book … that there's a God who loves you and accepts you and pursues you and forgives you and heals you and restores you. Yet when it comes to telling others about all that, we get nervous. We clam up. We worry it'll be awkward.

And it might be. That's the truth—sometimes conversations about God are awkward. But imagine an old-fashioned scale. On one side is you feeling awkward. On the other side is someone hearing that they, too, are loved and accepted and pursued, and that they can be forgiven and healed and restored.

What does that scale look like? Spoiler alert: the telling far outweighs you momentarily feeling awkward.

2. Sometimes we don't think long or hard enough about how others feel. Specifically those who are different. And sometimes all we can think about is how different we feel—and how not normal we are.

But in light of 1 Samuel 16:7, what does God think about? What does He see when He looks at the people He's made? What does He care about? And who does He want to use as He grows His kingdom?

> "But the LORD said to Samuel, 'Do not look on
> his appearance or on the height of his stature,
> because I have rejected him. For the LORD sees
> not as man sees: man looks on the outward
> appearance, but the LORD looks on the heart.'"
> 1 Samuel 16:7

3. It's easy to focus on suffering itself. But where in your own life, or in the lives of others, do you see God in the midst of pain and suffering?

33

Forgiveness: Andrew's Story

You will be hurt. It's unavoidable.

And we're not talking about the surface-level "ouch, I got a papercut" kind of hurt. We're talking about the type of hurt that doesn't go away with a Band-Aid. The kind that cuts you in the deepest place imaginable—your heart.

Sometimes heart wounds are unintentional: the result of an innocent tease gone too far, or the sting of a parent's offhand comment about your looks or your grades or your choices.

Sometimes heart wounds are intentional and aimed at doing the most damage possible: a jealous rumor that turns into widespread gossip or a scathing insult laced with harsh words.

Sometimes heart wounds are inflicted on someone else as a result of something **you** did or said.

Regardless of the specifics, heart wounds are difficult to overcome.

Hold that thought and consider Andrew.

We haven't talked about Andrew much. In the show, he's depicted as being the polar opposite of Simon. He's happy-go-lucky, always joking (and eating something, it seems), eager to please, and among the first to follow Jesus. In fact, Simon followed Jesus after Andrew made the introduction.

Season 3, Episode 1

But despite his good nature, Andrew's fear and anxiety got the better of him. He grew agitated—angry even—by the ever-increasing turmoil around him and looked for someone to blame. So, when Mary Magdalene returned to the group after falling back into her old ways, Andrew lashed out, yelled at her, and told her that the chaos and confusion were all her fault.

His words cut Mary deep.

Truth is, following Jesus doesn't prevent us from inflicting wounds upon each other. But God does offer medicine for those wounds, no matter their source or size. As Jesus was hanging in agony on the cross, He said one of the most astonishing things in all of history:

"Father, forgive them, for they do not know what they are doing" (Luke 23:34 NIV).

Forgive them, Jesus said, even as the murderous men divvied up His clothes.

And forgiveness is the antidote for heart wounds. In order to heal, you have to forgive those who've wounded you. And you must ask for forgiveness from those you've wounded.

But that's easier said than done, right? We tend to hold on to pain, which turns into a grudge, which turns into bitterness. Yet, when you forgive, the power those wounds hold over you begins to fade. Forgiveness actually frees you from the bondage of bitterness. Likewise, when you seek forgiveness from those you've wronged, you open your heart to the work God wants to do inside of you.

Perhaps the hurt that has been inflicted upon you goes deeper than anyone can imagine, and your heart bears scars from years of neglect or abuse. Perhaps you've endured so much hurt that it impacts the way you see the world around you. You will likely never forget these things.

So, let's be really clear: to forgive doesn't mean to forget, because forgetting isn't something we're usually capable of. But forgiveness does accomplish two things. First, it actually acknowledges you've been hurt deeply. Second, it prevents your pain from defining you.

It diminishes the power that your wounds hold over you.

After he heard the Sermon on the Mount, Andrew visited Mary Magdalene and asked for her forgiveness. In doing so, he unlocked something incredible, not only in himself, but also in Mary, who said, "This might be the first time someone has said sorry to me."

You will be hurt. It's unavoidable. But learning to forgive not only frees you from the power that heart wounds have, it also transforms your heart, making you more like the One you follow.

"Father, forgive them, for they do not know what they are doing" (Luke 23:34 NIV).

Pray

Father, You have forgiven my sins through the sacrifice Jesus made on the cross. Help me to forgive others in the same way. And give me the strength to seek forgiveness from those I've hurt too.

"And [Jesus] opened his mouth and taught them, saying: 'Blessed are the poor in spirit, for theirs is the kingdom of heaven. Blessed are those who mourn, for they shall be comforted. Blessed are the meek, for they shall inherit the earth. Blessed are those who hunger and thirst for righteousness, for they shall be satisfied. Blessed are the merciful, for they shall receive mercy. Blessed are the pure in heart, for they shall see God. Blessed are the peacemakers, for they shall be called sons of God. Blessed are those who are persecuted for righteousness' sake, for theirs is the kingdom of heaven' ... You have heard that it was said, 'You shall love your neighbor and hate your enemy.' But I say to you, Love your enemies and pray for those who persecute you, so that you may be sons of your Father who is in heaven. For he makes his sun rise on the evil and on the good, and sends rain on the just and on the unjust." Matthew 5:2–10, 43–45

Reflect

1. Why is forgiving so hard?

2. What hurts are you holding on to? Who do you need to forgive?

3. Who do you need to seek forgiveness from?

34

Family: Matthew's Story

Matthew is one of the most beloved characters in **The Chosen.** Maybe that's because he's easy to relate to—at some point in our lives, we've all felt the sting of not fitting in.

Season 3,
Episode 1

Matthew didn't even fit in with his own family. It was hard to watch the consequences unfold as his decision to collect taxes from Rome led to his father disowning him. Still, he continued to live his self-centered life as the wealthiest Israelite in town, further driving a wedge between him and his family.

No doubt, your circumstances are different from Matthew's, but the pain and isolation he felt are totally relatable. And here's the bottom line: hurts caused by family tend to hurt the most.

Of course, we don't get to pick our families; it's more like a game of cards where you don't have any control over the hand you've been dealt. Perhaps you were dealt an incredible hand with several wild draw-fours. Perhaps you were dealt a terrible hand with nothing but mismatched colors and numbers. Or perhaps you weren't dealt any hand at all since over 400,000 children are in foster care in America alone.

Here's the good news, though. Following Jesus moves your focus from the hand you've been dealt to how you play the game.

During the Sermon on the Mount, we saw Matthew overcome with emotion as the realization of Jesus's words set in:

"So if you are offering your gift at the altar and there remember that your brother has something against you, leave your gift there before the altar and go. First be reconciled to your brother, and then come and offer your gift" (Matthew 5:23–24).

It struck home for Matthew. Yes, his father disowned him. But Jesus's words helped Matthew see that he was also to blame. So, Matthew followed Jesus's instructions, and what resulted was one of the most touching moments in the show—father and son were reunited.

Reconciliation is forgiveness in action. It's an extension of the lesson Andrew learned in yesterday's devotion. Reconciliation happens when both people are able to forgive and move forward together.

You might not be in a place where you can reconcile with your family. You might not ever be. But the principle Jesus taught still applies.

Forgiveness and reconciliation mean you no longer consider the other person "in debt" to you. It means their actions no longer hold power over you. Regardless of what they do, regardless of what they say, **you** have chosen to follow Jesus into the freedom that forgiveness brings.

> Remember that line from the Lord's Prayer? "And forgive us our debts, as we also have forgiven our debtors." Matthew 6:12

That said, you're going to hear a couple voices preaching that family isn't worth it.

The first voice belongs to the culture. It shouts that **you** are the center of your universe. And that doesn't leave much room for family—unless, of course, they improve your self-worth. If not, families become disposable in the name of self-help.

The other voice comes from inside. "You don't understand me!" has been the rallying cry of children across countless generations. You've said it, or you've at least felt it. Your parents probably said it to their parents. Your kids will say it someday too, because that voice has been speaking that particular lie since Cain took up arms against his brother Abel.

> The story of Cain and Abel is found in Genesis 4.

But Jesus speaks too, and He says to forgive your family, just as He has forgiven you. When you do, you'll find that your heart and mind are no longer held hostage by family wounds. And that Jesus's love and forgiveness rush in, healing your wounds and guarding your heart in ways you couldn't have previously imagined.

Pray

Father, You created me, and that means You gave me my family. Help me learn what it means to forgive them, Father, in the small things and in the big things. Help me to not hold them in debt, just as You no longer hold me in Your debt. Help me forgive just as You have forgiven me.

Reflect

1. When you think of the "perfect" family, what comes to mind? And why doesn't the perfect family exist?

2. How have people in your family hurt you? Be specific. Own it. It's only when you're honest that you can (a) accept the hurt and then (b) forgive it.

3. How have you hurt others in your family? Be specific. Own it. It's only when you're honest that you can (a) apologize for the hurt and then (b) receive forgiveness.

35

Feeding 5,000: The Crowd's Story

Picture the scene: There are so many people here. More than you've ever seen in one place at one time. Which means there's so much to take in. It seems like every type of person imaginable (and after such a long, hot day, every kind of smell imaginable—ewww) is here listening to this one guy.

Season 3, Episode 1

You've managed to squeeze yourself close to the front of the crowd ... still a few rows of people away from the front, but close enough that you can hear everything being said.

And the things you've seen today! It doesn't make any sense. There's your neighbor, who needs a cane to walk from his house to the market—and now he's dancing like it's his wedding day. And the little blind girl who begs for money on the corner near your house ... she can't stop asking the people around her about the name of each new color she can suddenly see.

Could it be that this man isn't **just** a man? Could He actually be the Savior promised by the prophets so long ago? It sure seems that way, except that the revolution He's leading isn't what you—or anyone else—expected.

You haven't had time to think about it before now, but suddenly your stomach growls loud enough that a woman turns and looks at you, eyebrows raised. But it seems you're not the only one who's hungry—folks are starting to get restless, but no one wants to leave. You decide to stick it out for a little while longer. With every new healing, you think the whispers, that this rabbi from Nazareth is indeed the Messiah, might be true.

It's not long before the crowd grows from restless to grumbly. They all mill around looking for food. And your stomach has moved from growling to backflipping. You start to panic, realizing not only will there be no dinner for you tonight, there might not be any food tomorrow. Because this many hungry people will clear out all the food from every market within walking distance.

Then, commotion breaks out in front of you. One of Jesus's followers—Jonah's son Andrew, of all people (your dad used to buy fish from their family)—has brought someone to Jesus. Andrew asks, "There is a boy here who has five barley loaves and two fish, but what are they for so many?" (John 6:9). Your mouth starts watering just at the sight of bread and fish. But hope quickly turns to dismay … That's definitely not enough food for a crowd so large.

Jesus asks everyone to sit down anyway. He takes the little boy's loaves and fish and says a blessing over them. The next thing you know, Andrew himself is holding a basket full of fish out to you … he's shouting, you're shouting, everyone's shouting—WHAT … IS … HAPPENING?? It's just fish and bread, but it's the best meal you've ever had. And you're sharing it with thousands of others.

Five loaves plus two fish equals a meal for more than five thousand. It's impossible math. Nevertheless, a little boy and his little offering in the hands of Jesus do indeed result in very big things.

Out of the corner of your eye, you spot Jesus. There's a little smile pulling up the corners of His mouth as He watches the celebration. Then He sees you. Not the crowd, not the person next to you. You. And He does a very Jesus kind of thing.

He winks at you.

Pray

Father, You are the great Provider. You are the One who cares for us. You are the One who feeds the multitudes. Help me to bring my loaves and fish to You.

> Our loaves and fish = whatever we offer to Jesus, no matter how small. Our time, our talent, our money, our love ... we bring what we have and trust Him to multiply and use it.

Reflect

1. Read John 6:1–14. Why do you think Jesus let the people get so hungry?

2. Why is it significant that Jesus fed five thousand people instead of letting them go look for food on their own?

3. What loaves and fish can you bring to Jesus?

30

Don't Let Me Go: Simon's Story

D on't let me go."

The words of a man who had seen Jesus do impossible things. A man who had done impossible things himself in Jesus's name.

"Don't let me go."

The words of a man with such audacious faith that he climbed over the edge of a boat in the middle of a storm. A man who, just a moment ago, was doing the most impossible thing of all—walking on water to Jesus.

Season 3,
Episode 8

"Don't let me go."

A man who—despite experiencing many different kinds of miracles—still found himself sinking as the waves of doubt and fear crashed over him.

"Jesus, don't let me go."

Those are powerful and important words.

The first scripture we shared in this book was from Isaiah 43: "Fear not, for I have redeemed you; I have called you by name, you are mine. When you pass through the waters, I will be with you; and through the rivers, they shall not overwhelm you."

It's not a question of **if** the waters around you will rise. They will. It's not a question of **if** the waters will sometimes overwhelm. They will. It's not a question of **if** you'll feel yourself sinking at some point. You will. And, like Simon Peter, your natural instinct will be to focus on rising waters and scary storms instead of Jesus. You'll be tempted to take your eyes off the One who called you out of the boat and onto those very waves.

Bottom line: life can be really hard sometimes, and it will toss you around like a little boat in the middle of a raging storm. You will question. You will doubt. You will experience the kind of fear that threatens to pull you under the waves.

But the real question is, what will you **do** when it happens?

"Don't let me go."

The words of someone willing to trust Jesus.

"Don't let me go."

The words of someone brave enough to climb over the edge of a boat in the middle of a storm because Jesus is the One waiting in the waves.

"Don't let me go."

Your words when you think you might be sinking.

But this famous Bible story isn't just about Simon walking on the water. It's not about his bravery or even his faith. This story is about Jesus. Because He's the God who walks on water.

And He will never let you go.

Pray

Jesus, don't let me go.

Reflect

1. Read Matthew 14:22–33. Why do you think the disciples were so afraid? What's **your** first instinct when things feel out of control?

2. Why did Jesus let Peter sink instead of just keeping him on top of the water? Why did Jesus wait for him to ask for help?

3. What causes you to take your eyes off Jesus? What might help you **keep** your eyes on Jesus?

GUIDED GROUP DISCUSSION

1. No one follows Jesus perfectly. Sooner or later we all get anxious or fearful or prideful or sinful in any number of ways—and we get hurt and we inflict hurt upon others. With all that in mind, why is it so important to follow Jesus's example of forgiveness? How does forgiving others help heal our own hearts? How would cultivating a culture of forgiveness inside the church entice others to want to follow Jesus too?

2. Why is it so important to bring our loaves and fish to God? By "loaves and fish," we mean whatever gift or offering you have to bring, no matter how small or inconsequential you think it is. Maybe you're good at being kind and encouraging to others. Maybe you're good at math and can help someone who isn't. Maybe you saved a little extra money from that summer job and are feeling a pull to be generous. Maybe you've noticed your next-door neighbor is a lonely old lady who never has visitors.

Whatever it is, bring your small offering to the One who multiplied a little boy's loaves and fish.

3. The Bible uses the picture of storms and waves to depict our struggles. We all have storms; we all experience moments that feel out of control and scary. But what does Isaiah 43:1–2 say about our storms? What does Simon's experience of walking on the water, then sinking, then being pulled out of the water again by Jesus teach us about the One we follow?

> "Fear not, for I have redeemed you; I have called
> you by name, you are mine. When you pass
> through the waters, I will be with you; and through
> the rivers, they shall not overwhelm you."
> Isaiah 43:1–2

About the Authors

Jeremiah Smith loves his wife and four kiddos, the Chicago Bears, and leading marketing for *The Chosen*. He's had some fun stops along the way: three years of Greek, being a pastor, and branding for the world's largest company.

Amanda Jenkins is an author, speaker, and the lead creator of *The Chosen's* additional content. Her husband, **Dallas Jenkins**, directed and produced over a dozen feature and short films before creating *The Chosen*, currently one of the most viewed TV shows in the world. They live in Texas with their four children.